Prisoner In Another Man's Castle

Collection

Douglas R. Townsend

PRISONER IN ANOTHER MAN'S CASTLE
COLLECTION

Contents

Dedication

My wife Mae,

Our oldest daughter Vista,

Our youngest daughter Vileta,

And our granddaughter Vista Roshell

Foreword

I grew up on a cotton farm in Neshoba County, Mississippi. I was a very shy person. Sometimes I would be at school all day and not speak to anyone. I never liked for people to interrupt when I was trying to talk.

To prevent this, I got paper and pen and began to write. My pen never would interrupt me while I was mediating.

Many years have gone by. However, I am still very bashful and timid. It is just a part of me.

You will find country atmosphere throughout my writings. I hope you will enjoy this book.

Chapter One

Prisoner In Another Man's Castle

Appreciation

To Castle of Deliverance and This Other Castle

This allegory is based on a true story. The feelings and emotions are real. The names were changed to protect the innocent and the guilty. May this story shine a light in many hearts and give them a new and better direction in life.

Characters

Prisoner In Another Man's Castle

While bound with chains here in this dark, cold pit, I cry rivers of tears. Being weakened and press down by the enemy, I have no power to free myself. Mentally I am exhausted. I feel that many invisible swords pierce my heart, each representing people I had let down over the years. Knowing that I had failed myself, I begin to ponder how I came to this place, deep into this castle, deep into this damp and dreary pit. I am not able to free my hands from the chains that hold me firmly.

Did anyone know where I was? That is, anyone who really cares? Evil spirits torment me in the night while sleep flees from my eyes. My body feels numb, my eyes grow dim from crying. I have lost all hope of ever escaping this pit.

Miserably in body, mind, and spirit, I begin to ask myself questions. How did I get here? How did I become a prisoner without even realizing what was happening to me? What could I have done to prevent this tragedy in my life? Will I ever know freedom again?

My mind reflects back years ago, when I was living freely in a land so fair. A land with many hills covered with beautiful trees. Down in the valley lay a clear refreshing lake. The cool breeze would quietly blow over the hills. The trees would wave their tender branches at each other as the wind slowly flowed over the country side. I could see a beautiful castle, surrounded by sweet smelling flowers. Joy and laughter came from this castle. Around her were many small hills. Here trees would shade the weary while her flowers would refresh the lonely. It was a delight every time I visited this lovely Castle Of Innocence.

To my left, across the lush valley, I could also see an old castle. It had need of much repair. His yard was unkempt and ragged. Once his fields were plowed and children's laughter filled his colorful halls. If you visited this Castle Of Courage, you would always receive a welcome there.

Behind me was Another Man's Castle which stood tall and strong. The birds would whisper in the air and warn of anyone approaching Another Man's Castle. She was surrounded by tall rolling hills and deep valleys. You would get a welcome there; however, inside her walls could be heard screams for help. She would tell us that it was just the wind blowing through her halls and doorways decorated with hundreds of chimes. This castle was filled with many strange sounds in the darkness of the night.

Just over the northern hillside stood the Castle Of Adventure, who always reached out her loving arms to give you a welcome hug. She would adventure out across the rolling hills, looking for something new and exciting to do.

Oh, by the way, I must tell you about the castle that stood by the brook. Often I would stroll over and visit this Castle Of Pleasure. She was always looking for things to do that would give her lots of pleasure. You would have enjoyed her company.

Then there is the Castle Of Deliverance. He stood on top of the northern hill which was the highest in our fair land. He mostly kept to himself unless someone got in trouble and called on him for help. You could always depend on the

Castle of Deliverance. He was a gentleman, very kind and thoughtful.

This Other Castle stood alone in the south country. I never made my acquaintance with anyone there. She stayed mostly to herself and was seen by only a seldom few who passed by. Word was that she was very religious and holy.

My castle was simple and quite empty. I lived in the Castle of Embarrassment all by myself. I never talked much, so I had only a few friends. Some people called me a loner. Maybe they were right.

As I recall the sunny days of long ago, some memories make me happy, while others sadden my heart. All the memories are tightly woven together, forming me into who I really am today.

One early morning I was awoken by a rooster crowing on the fence. The sun's rays were quietly creeping across the orange and red sky. Springing out of bed joyfully, I was excited. The smell of bacon and eggs filled the kitchen. It was prepared by hands of love and served with care and concern by the faithful cook. The smell of fresh perked coffee flowed through the house like a cool breeze. After eating breakfast, I took a stroll across the grassy meadow, as I often did. I enjoyed looking across the distance at the Castle Of Innocence. Oh, she was beautiful.

I had been living in this fair land for a while before I became acquainted with Castle of Innocence. I began to look across her smooth, small hills, covered with many sweet smelling flowers. Even though her castle was a distance away from where I lived, I could smell her lovely flowers. It excited me to gaze across her soft, gentle rolling hills.

Even though I had made my acquaintance with most of the other castles in our fair land, there was something that drew me to the Castle Of Innocence. After watching the sun rise over her beautiful steeple and gently expose her beauty into the cool breeze that surrounded her castle, I felt I had to make my acquaintance with her. It took some time before I could get the courage to go over and knock on her door.

It seemed to be a perfect day. The sun's rays glittered through the leaves on the trees, birds singing in their branches, and beautiful butterflies fluttering from flower to flower. The breeze was soft and cool with a few clouds floating across the blue sky. I strolled across the grassy hills and stood before her door, hoping that she would invite me in.

Finally the moment came. Standing in front of her door I slowly raised my right hand and tapped on the door. No movement came from inside. I knocked once more. *Knock, knock, knock.* The castle door slowly began to open. Standing in the hallway was Innocence. I could not believe my eyes. She was breathtaking. Silently I stood for a moment, not expecting to see such beauty. Her blue eyes looked at me while her long, light brown hair waved at me in the wind. Her face held a warm smile while her eyes seem to search my thoughts.

You should have seen her sweet, rosy lips as they said, "Good morning. May I help you?"

My heart melted in warmth like butter on a hot stove. I tried to speak, but no sound came from my lips. After trying a second time, I was able to say, "Good morning. I would like to make your acquaintance, madam, most honorable Innocence. I live across the valley in the Castle Of

Embarrassment. It is my pleasure to make your acquaintance."

"It's also my pleasure. I have noticed you looking this way quite often. Will you please come in for a cup of hot tea?" spoke Innocence.

I moved quickly through the doorway, still gazing at her beauty. Reaching out to take her hand, a strange feeling came over me that I had never felt before. How can you explain such a wonderful, powerful, binding emotion that flowed through my entire being? It was like a strong magnet pulling something from her into me, a powerful bond strong enough to last a lifetime.

As the custom was in our fair land, I slowly raised her hand to my lips to give Innocence a greeting kiss. As my lips touched her hand, it seemed as though a thousand springs of refreshing water sprang up and filled my entire being with excitement. She stood speechless, her eyes gazing into mine. I could feel her drawing something out of me, and it penetrated her heart with warmth.

What is going on inside me? I wondered.

While still looking into her eyes, I lowered Innocence's right hand and slowly let it go. No, I did not want to let go. I had rather held her hand forever. What a wonderful, captivating feeling that came over me that first day I met her and kissed her hand, a warm feeling that I shall never forget all the days of my life. This feeling has always been part of me. After visiting for a long time, I bid her farewell for the day. I slowly walked across the valley and up the hill to my Castle Of Embarrassment. I was feeling so very wonderful.

The next day I decided to stroll over to the Castle Of Pleasure. She lived down by the cool brook. She was always looking for some kind of pleasure, nothing bad, but often mischievous. We would often visit other castles and gather up a few people so we could have fun. While strolling over the nearby hills, we would share lots of pleasure. On this particular day, we took my chariot and rode over the mountain to the next village. I let her drive my chariot. This excited her for she received a lot of pleasure from driving it. Bumping along the way, we shared stories about our neighbors. The sun had almost set when we arrived back at the Castle of Pleasure. What a wonderful day, spending it with a friend. When I arrived home, darkness had crept over the hills of our fair land.

A few days later, Castle Of Adventure invited me to come over to her castle to play a few games of cards. I arrived in the middle of the afternoon. She met me at the door with a lovely welcoming smile. Adventure was the daughter of Another Man's Castle. Often Another Man's Castle would join us in a game. She liked playing cards also. However, on this night it was only Castle of Adventure and me. She brought in a table and two chairs and set them in the middle of the guest chamber. The game began, and so did the rain. The rain fell for two hours; however, our game went on for nearly three hours. We enjoyed a night of playing, talking, and romancing.

About ten that night, the clouds cleared away. Deciding to take a chariot ride, we hooked up the horse and began to ride. The stars were out and the moon was shining brightly. The chariot moved slowly along the high ridge in the moonlight. Adventure moved close to me and laid her head on my shoulder. This felt very good. Exciting was the ride with Adventure in the moonlight, under the stars. About one in the morning, I arrived back home. It had been a great, romantic night.

Almost every week some of the neighbors would get together and visit the Castle Of Courage. Across the flowing valley we would go, often early in the morning. When we arrived, he would welcome us saying, "Come on in for a great meal." A table of delicious food would always be waiting our arrival. Here we would get strength for another day. We would also get good council and encouragement. Courage made everyone feel welcomed. Biding him farewell for the day, he would say, "Hope to see you next week."

One day I became very sick while doing some repairs to my Castle of Embarrassment. The days were long, and the nights very lonely. One night, to my surprise, a knock rang out on my door. Hobbling to the door, I slowly opened it. There stood Castle Of Courage. With a welcome I invited him in. He sat with me for a while. I was greatly encouraged by his wisdom and the delicious meal he brought me. As he walked out the door to go home, I felt reinvigorated. His visit with me meant so much that night.

I felt much better but not well. Another neighbor made a surprise visit. When I opened my door, it refreshed my heart to see Castle Of Innocence standing there. I quickly invited her in. Taking her right hand, I lifted it to my lips as a gesture of welcoming. I led Innocence to my guest chamber and we sat on a sofa. I could feel her warmth as it flowed out to me. Knowing by now that she really cared for me, I moved closer to her on the sofa. As we talked for hours, we became fully wrapped with everlasting love for each other, a love that only death can take away.

Innocence's inner beauty shone to me. Sitting beside me was a beautiful girl who had a body and heart of innocence. She was full of passion and love overflowing. If an angel has ever been sent to me, I am sure it would be named Innocence. While sitting so close to her, our hearts formed a bond that could not be pulled apart, except one of our hearts should be broken. I could not image that ever happening. No, not to a lady who had so much to give. Eleven o'clock arrived too quickly, and Innocence had to say good night. While embracing, we shared a good night kiss. It lit a flame in my heart that has never gone out. Away she went. I shall never forget that night. The next day, I felt fine. So I went about my usual daily tasks while being filled with love and strength.

Sometime later in the fall when the leaves were taking their flight to the ground, my curiosity got the best of me. I began to wonder what was going on inside Another Man's Castle. I suppose it was her tall rolling hills that stood on each side of her deep valley that really got my attention. Often when she would play cards with Castle Of Adventure, her daughter, and me, I would find myself gazing at Castle. When eye contact was made, I began to have some strange feelings. I suppose it was feelings of curiosity, definite not love. But what was it?

One day, to my surprise, Another Man asked me to carry his castle on a chariot ride and teach her how to drive it. Well, I thought that maybe this way I can find out more about what was going on in Another Man's Castle. Another Man was too busy in sports to teach his castle how to drive. So I told him that I would do the honor of teaching her how to drive the chariot.

The next day we went on a short ride all alone. Everything went well. I enjoyed the ride, so I went again. This time Castle was not pleased just to drive, but she moved close to me while we were on the trails. Soon we began staying close every time we went out.

Castle suggested taking a mountain trail one day. I thought, why not? Another Man did not care which road we traveled on. Castle's territories included deep valleys and tall, rolling hills. Her mountainous hills reached high and got the attention of a lot of people who were traveling through our fair land. So up the mountain trail we went that day.

After two hours journeying up the trail, Castle said, "This would be a good place to stop and rest for a while."

While letting the horse cool off, she moved very close to me. Then she asked if I would like to take a hike up one of her mountains, even to the peak. This trip started a new journey in my life. Little did I know how much she liked the rides and hiking up her mountain trails.

It did not concern Another Man for Castle and me to be gone all day. This gave him time to do what he wanted to. As the next few weeks passed, Castle and I would take our usual ride up one mountain all the way to the peak, then down the mountain, across the deep valley and up the other mountain peak. It became a fun game running up the mountain trails, up this mountain, across the valley, and up the other mountain. Sometimes Castle would want me to travel slowly when we crossed the deep valley. I continued playing her game. While parked on the empty private trails, she said that it would make her warm and excited as we climbed up the mountains.

Little did I know what was really happening while we journeyed over her hills and mountains so tall? I soon was enjoying this game as much as Castle was. I began to look forward to our time together, close together. Soon we were so close we seemed like one person. It began to possess my mind. All my attention was focused on the time I could be with her and play her mountain climbing game.

Eventually Another Man became concerned about the time Castle and I were spending together. He heard about the mountain games that we were involved in playing. So he asked me to stop coming to Another Man's Castle and to stop playing games with his castle. Did I listen to him? No, by this time the mountain hikes and games had taken possession of me. I wanted to obey him and stop, but I could not.

Sometimes Adventure would go with Castle and me on our trail rides. She caught on to the games Castle and I were playing. However Adventure never played the games with us. She kept quiet about it and never told her father.

One day, while Another Man was not at home, Castle invited me to come inside her castle. While there, she showed me the guest room, the family room, and last the bed chamber. It was large with dim lights. The bed was broad and covered with a spread of many wonderful colors. The headboard was made of soft woven chains. The foot rail was wrapped with exciting soft blue velvet. When the covers were turned back, the bed had an inviting, silent whisper to it. The mattress was very soft and warm, carrying the scent of many pleasures, a place where most men could enjoy spending a night.

While in the castle that day, we also entered into her private chamber which included a very dark room downstairs. In this lower, dark room you could join her in the most pleasurable game. In this game, you would go in and out of the deep, dark pit as many times as you wanted to. Then she would shut the door and the object of the game was to see if you could get out by yourself.

During the next several months, I would visit Another Man's Castle two or three times each week. Now the games were not played out on the mountain trails, but in her private, personal chambers. Another Man told me to stay away and stop playing her games. However, I would not stop because I could not stop. It was like some evil spirit had taken control of me, and I could not get loose. I wanted to stay away, but I could not. Castle had caught me in a net with her games. Now I was bound and could not get loose. It started out with hours of pleasure each week. Her games slowly bound me with chains. Castle and her evil spirit would not let me go.

When I first started visiting Another Man's Castle, I was also spending time with Castle of Innocence. In my first few months of visiting Another Man's Castle, Innocence and I saw one another every few days. I enjoyed her company very much. My love for her kept me visiting her often. We were so happy together. Following the trails over her small hills we would share laughter together.

While I was spending many hours with Another Man's Castle each week, her spirit of power began to take my time and attention away from Innocence. Innocence knew that something bad was going on. She talked to me a number of times and begged me to stay away from Another Man's

Castle. Her love was tugging at my heart, while Castle's pleasure was pulling hard on me to lavish myself in her games of lust. Who will win? Who will lose? This is a position that no man should ever permit himself to get into. This is a battle of evil against good.

One night Innocence invited me to go with her to visit her parents. During the visit we were served a delicious supper. It was a pleasure meeting her parents. They were as nice and polite as Innocence. At this time in our relationship, I never would have believed that some evil plot would pull us apart. I thought that Innocence and me would always be together to share our lives for many years. Often the midnight moonlight would find us sitting under the maple tree while gazing into one another's eyes. Deep within our hearts, we found a love and compassion that would never cease or pass away. As I held her hands, a strong, warm feeling passed through my entire being. It knitted us so very close together, like someone knitting a scarf together, never to be taken apart. Her touch was soft and warm. I shall never forget it.

A thousand times over, I wish that I would have recognized the evil, lustful scheme that Another Man's Castle was secretly planning. How unlearned and inexperienced I was at that time. It cost me more than I could ever pay. I also lost something that I could not ever have again. It almost destroyed Innocence.

Soon, Innocence began to feel that something was wrong. It did not take her long to figure it out. In the meantime, I was visiting Another Man's Castle more and more. Castle and I were taking more hikes and chariot rides together that Innocence heard about. She would often walk to the top of one of her hills. While gazing across the valley, she would see me with Castle. Oh, how much did it hurt Innocence! Lust had begun to blind my emotions and feelings.

In the next few weeks Innocence's heart began to hurt very badly. I had allowed the power of lust to blind my eyes so that I was losing sight of my real love, Innocence, my dear Innocence. How could any man allow lust to overpower real love? My attention turned to Another Man's Castle. I soon got to the place where I could only see her way. I could not look in another direction. Soon I became totally possessed with the power of lust for Castle. It weaved a web around my heart to where I could not feel Innocence's love any more. I lost complete control of my feelings, emotions, and life.

All this pain and hurt came about because I allowed the power of lust to take control of my life. I got to the place where all I wanted to do was to be with Another Man's Castle. Another Man asked me to stop visiting his castle, but I was so overpowered by lust, I could not stop. I kept going on the chariot rides with her, up the mountains and down the other side, up one mountain peak and then to another peak. We would often go deep down into the valley and enter into a deep cave of mystery. I took lots of ventures in this mysterious cave.

The games played on the mountain seemed to be the real freedom in life. However, when I began to visit in Castles' private chambers and entering into the lower, dark room, this is when I lost control in every way. There we would play her games of pleasure. After a while, I began to want to stop, but she overpowered me. This is when Castle bound me with chains and snapped the lock tight. No one in our fair land ever saw me much anymore because I had become a prisoner to Castle. Here in this cool, dark pit in her lower chamber, I realized that Castle had overpowered me, bound me, and made me her slave of sports. For her, she still played her games in the lower chamber; however, I moved like a puppet. It is hard to do anything when you are bound with an evil power of lust. This could very well be the strongest evil power in the universe.

For Innocence, the next two or three years were very hard. During these years while I was with Another Man's Castle, Innocence was near us at work. As we cultivated and worked the fields, we all worked close together. The fields joined each other on the rolling hills. While preparing the soil and planting the seed, Innocence would see Castle and me working side by side. Innocence had to suffer this hurt and pain almost every day. All through the summer this went on. In the fall at harvest time nothing had changed.

Innocence looked on from her small farm on the hill. How much she wanted my love and affection. Because lust had bound me so tightly, her love could not penetrate my heart. I would see Innocence almost every day with my eyes. My heart could no longer feel her love and longing she had for me. It was like my heart had turned to stone.

As all the farmers worked in the summer sun, it was very hot and dry. When it was time to go to the shade and take a break, Innocence was desperately lonely and hurt. Castle and I would always rest in the shade together, sitting close while talking and blinded in lust. We were not ashamed of who saw us or who disapproved of our actions. Innocence had to see what was going on. She painfully watched our closeness melt away. It melted like an ice cube on a hot summer day. Innocence was losing me. It drove sharp pains through her heart as she watched day after day. Her mind and heart were tormented from all that she saw and knew week after week, month after month. Innocence was ashamed and disrespected because of the way I showed her no love or attention. For the next several months, this was the normal routine for Innocence.

During those years, no one came to me to give me council. It was like no one cared about my direction in life. As Innocence watched on, it was like someone standing on a lonely hill, watching her most loved castle go up in a fire and smoke, losing all she owned and wanted. She spent many nights weeping and crying, but sleep would not come. Innocence dreaded to see the mornings when it was time to go to the fields. There across the fields, she would watch her most treasured castle fade away into a lustful fog. In the mist, she eventually lost sight of me. However, her love for me never faded.

I still remember how Innocence pleaded with me to stop visiting Another Man's Castle. While Innocence's heart was breaking in pieces, she tried reaching out to me in every way she knew how. It was like my heart had turned to stone. She once built her world around me, but like a fool, I tore it down. I had a trophy of purest gold, but I let it slip through my fingers, never being able to pick her up again.

We finally came to our last date. I remember it as if it was last night. Innocence and I had gone for a chariot ride in the moonlight. She was as beautiful as an angel. Her long, light brown hair was waving in the cool breeze. Those loving blue eyes were pleading with me. I felt her hands quivering in mine because her heart was hurting so much, so very much. As we arrived back at her castle, Innocence turned in the seat where she was facing me. Because she was in so much pain, it was very difficult for her to talk. With her sweet lips she begged me not to turn from her, not to leave her. Over and over Innocence pleaded and begged me not to go from her.

I have not the words in my vocabulary to share what Innocence was feeling, the pain, the hurt, the grief, the loneness, the pressure, the emptiness, the coming apart of her heart as I drove away that night on our last date. It was like I was ripping her life from her body. I did not only break Innocence's heart, I broke it up into many pieces, and those into tinier pieces. I crushed her precious heart under my feet, grinding it into the dirt along with all the embarrassment and shame that I gave her. The reason that I was turning away from Innocence and to whom I was going brought her disrespect, dishonor, shame, embarrassment, and an everlasting hurt. Oh, how much it hurt her.

My leaving Innocence opened a flood gate of rivers of tears and sobs. For months and months her tears flowed. Her crying could be heard across the small hills and valleys. How could anyone live with a heart crushed into so many pieces? No angel, no beautiful girl ever deserved to be hurt this badly as Innocence was hurt. Lust had stopped up my ears to where I could not hear her pitiful cries and moans. It was only years later when I began to hear them with my heart and feel the hurt that I gave her.

The next several months found Innocence pressed down in pain, tears, and depression. The one she loved had been lost. Feeling empty, lonely, and rejected, she fell into a deep, depressed state of mind. This feeling soon overtook her emotionally. The tears would not stop. The pain would not go away. Innocence was reaching out for someone she could never hold again. Her emotions overpowered reality. Innocence's mind was losing its sense of directions. Because of her being so badly wounded in heart and spirit, Innocence had to be put away in a mental care unit for several months. When I let lust overpowered me, I had no idea how much it would hurt Innocence and other people. My lustful desires almost destroyed a beautiful and loving young girl's mind, heart, and life.

During my lustful years, Innocence never lost her love for me. Shortly after we first began to share our love, I gave her a gift. During those hard years for her, she kept the gift. While working in the field one day, Innocence came over the hill where I was. At this time she gave back to me the gift. She had accept the fact that we would not share our love and life together. It was a painful, heart-breaking moment for Innocence as she walked away that day.

There was a short time toward the end of the lustful journey when I began to reach out toward Innocence. I wanted her love and presence again. Often I would go close to where she was in the field, park, or some other place. A strong desire to be with her began to come alive again. But it was too late. Another Man's Castle noticed and locked me in her castle.

While a prisoner, I never knew how Castle of Deliverance heard where I was nor why Deliverance would be concerned about me. A worthless nobody was I, sitting here in this dark pit, bound with these chains of lust. I barely had strength to raise my head and look up. Regardless of my bondage of evil, Deliverance began to put together a plan to free me from this miserable pit. He considered many people in our fair land to accomplish this hard task. After some time, he found just the right person for the job. Everyone had strength and power in some areas. However, to deliver me it would take a person with a special talent, strength, and courage.

One day there was a knock on This Other Castle's door. When she opened the door, what a surprise! There stood Deliverance. Some people in our fair land hardly knew Deliverance. It was different with This Other Castle. She knew him very well. In fact, Deliverance was her very best friend. They often talked privately about many things in her life and the life of others.

This Other Castle said, "Please come in and make yourself comfortable."

As Deliverance took a seat, he quietly looked around the clean, well-kept room. No spots of dirt could be seen. There was not one unclean room in her castle. Other Castle spent much time studying the cleaning rules to make sure her whole castle was kept spotless and refreshing.

Deliverance broke the silence. "Other Castle, I have a challenging job that needs to be done. I have considered others; however, you are the most qualified of all the available people in this fair land."

"Oh, tell me what it is," spoke Other Castle.

"Other Castle," said Deliverance, "I must first tell you why you have been chosen for this most important task. It is because of your training and discipline to be a brave warrior for me. You have much training on how to handle the two-edged sword. There is nothing any sharper; however, one must know well how to handle it properly. In training, you always wear the breastplate so it will shield off any darts or sword used against you. You remember that the skills of preparation are very important. You have studied every detail of your sword. You know what every curve and line on it is for. See, Other Castle, I need a very special, highly trained person for this task. After considering many others, I have chosen you, Other Castle."

"Oh, what task could possibly be so important?" asked Other Castle.

Castle Of Deliverance said, "I do not deliver people from trouble and prisons all by myself. In delivering them, I choose qualified knights to fight in the battle with me. I equip my warriors with power, strength, direction, and wisdom. I also show them the battle strategy. I have a powerful captain over all my warriors who will carefully guide them in each battle."

By now, Other Castle's curiosity was really busy wondering what the task was. She said, "Come on. Tell me what you want me to do."

"Okay," said Deliverance, "This is what I want you to do. There is a young man that you have never met. He has allowed himself to be wrapped in a tangled web that he cannot free himself from. I have chosen him to be a soldier. He is now bound with chains, deep within a dark, cold pit. He really wants out; however, the chain of lust has bound him so tight that he has no strength to get himself out. He once was a castle of honor and respect. But when lust is welcomed into one's castle, lust will spread like a flood of water. Soon it blinds his eyes and dulls his hearing. Then it destroys feelings and emotions. Finally it binds him with the evil chains of lust. It will enslave him and cast him into an everlasting pit. He can never be set free, except I send a strong, brave soldier of faith to overpower the evil spirit and set him free.

"Other Castle, this is your assignment. I will give you further instructions as you need them. Arise, and march forward immediately. To battle you must go with love in your heart. I will be with you each step. I will not leave you alone. My captain will also go with you. March forward and do not retreat. Remember the power that is in your sword. Nothing is sharper. Be at ease."

At this, Deliverance dismissed himself. Other Castle put on her shoes and her breastplate. The shield was placed on her arm. The sword was carefully lifted and slipped into its holster. She marched forward on her way to conquer the task set before her. Other Castle did not ask why. She took the task by simple faith in Deliverance's assignment and wisdom.

It is dark and cold down here in this pit. I think it may be early in the morning. Light is something I seldom see anymore. Pain wants to rip apart my body. My mind is tortured by some evil power. Often I cry out for help, but no one hears me. My voice echoes back to me with screams of fear. The chains of lust share an evil laugh of mockery while spilling strange torments over me. I could have screamed for death to take me away. But for some unknown reason, I never do. All I have to do is call for Black Death, and he would have come and carried me away. I don't want to get out that way, but I have no idea how I might be set free. How much I yearn to be delivered from this evil pit. Why did I ever permit myself to become a slave to the evil spirit of lust?

What! Listen! I heard something! What did I hear? The door squeaks as it slowly opened. I see a flicker of light coming toward me. Soft footsteps are approaching me. They do not sound evil. What could this mean? I then hear a sweet, soft voice whisper to me.

She says, "I have come to set you free."

She reaches out with one hand, taking hold of the chain while holding a light in her other hand. I think, will I soon be free? The moment she touches the chains another door loudly swings open. Swiftly, someone came into the chamber to the edge of the pit. It was Another Man's Castle. She has in her hand a spear of Death.

Quickly Castle gives the spear to her strongest evil spirit and says, "Kill the intruder."

The one with the soft, sweet voice draws her sword swiftly. The battle is on. I can hear the clang of sword and spear. It is too dark for me to see what is taking place. I can see her little flickering light burning; she never lets go of that light. If she drops her light she will be defeated in the darkness. She has to walk in the light every moment. I can hear screams as the battle becomes intense.

All at once I hear a voice say, "In the name of Deliverance, you shall fall."

The sharp two-edged sword slices through the evil spirit. Falling, the evil spirit quietly lays on the floor. Quickly, with one hard blow, the sword comes down on the chains of lust, and the chains fall to the floor.

The girl with the soft voice takes me by the right hand and says, "We must go. You are free, yes, free indeed."

We quickly leave Another Man's Castle for the last time. I never look back. I never will want to again.

Other Castle and I quickly go over to the Castle Of Deliverance. Together we give thanks to Deliverance for setting me free. Deliverance gives us a special gift, a gift of love for one another. Other Castle is told by Deliverance that she is to love, protect, guard, strengthen, and walk with me for many years. He tells her that her task is only partly over. She is to continue her assignment with me until the final sunset.

After some time, Innocence regains her control of mind and direction in life. She marries and gives birth to a son. The last time I hear anything about Innocence, she, her husband, and her son are doing fine. Only time will reveal how well her heart has mended from the years of sadness and how many scars still remain from my breaking her heart so badly.

After I have been married for several years to Dove, it is like a numb hand without feeling begins to wake up and receive feeling again. That is when I begin to hear Innocence's tears and feel her pain in my heart. Then, in my night dreams I look for Innocence for many years, but cannot find her. After a long time I finally find her but cannot touch her. After a number of more years I finally touch her and hug her in a night dream, saying nothing to her. In my night dreams Innocence is usually at a distance and soon disappears. Maybe sometime in the future in my night dreams, I will be able to talk to her and offer my apology. I yearn to ask her to forgive me for breaking her heart, for causing so many tears, pain, dishonor, and disrespect. Then my night dreams about her might go away. However, my love for Innocence will never go away.

Other Castle and I are still walking together in perfect love as man and wife. Thanks to Other Castle and Castle of Deliverance, I am now free, yes, free indeed. Never again will I become a prisoner in Another Man's Castle.

Chapter Two

Dreams

The following dreams are real dreams that Castle of Embarrassment had about Castle of Innocence. They were dreamed over a number of years. They are not made up, and were not changed from the original dreams. There were many other dreams before Embarrassment started recording them. Almost all the dreams before being recorded included Embarrassment searching for Innocence. He could not get close to her when Embarrassment did sometimes find her in the dreams. These real dreams are dated but not altered.

NUMBER ONE
First Part of September, 2012

I dreamed that I, Embarrassment, saw Innocence behind a church pulpit making a speech, but I could not understand what she was saying. When she would finish with a page of notes, she would drop it on the floor. I would pick the notes up; however, I could not read them without Innocence's permission. I could not understand what she was saying. After Innocence finished her speech, she walked among the people. She never gave me permission to read the notes. We looked toward one another, but never spoke a word to one another. While making eye contact, we communicating that we both were hoping that we could get together again. Innocence was dressed in a red dress. Then I woke up from the dream.

NUMBER TWO
September 25, 2012

In my dream, I saw a large ice cube that was bigger than a house. It was floating down a river. Innocence and I were there. We were trying to miss the large cube of ice as it went by us. Innocence and I met while in this process of trying to miss the large ice cube. When we met, we kissed one another. She was dressed in red. I woke up.

NUMBER THREE
October 2, 2012

Around 3:00 A.M. I dreamed that I saw Innocence for the first time in a very long time. I came in from some place and she was there. Innocence came close to where I was and recognized me. The next day she came back. This time I was down on my knees working, doing something. I asked her for a date. Innocence never answered me. Then I knew what her answer was even though she spoke not a word. "Yes" was her answer. I woke up.

NUMBER FOUR
October 18, 2012

In this dream I, Embarrassment, was in the same house with Innocence. Innocence, I, and two friends were lying down on the same bed. Hanky-panky was not going on. I asked one of my friends to get up and get me a pair of pants to put on. He did not want to get up. I asked Innocence to push him out of the bed so he would get my pants. She did not say anything; however she did push him out of the bed. The dream ended.

NUMBER FIVE
N0VEMBER 12, 2012

I dreamed that I asked a young teenage boy if he knew where Innocence lived. He said that he did and would show me where she lived. I found her and her husband. This was the first time that I dreamed that Innocence had a husband. Her husband said that he did not care if Innocence and I spent some time alone there at their house. So we did, but I do not know what we talked about. The dream ended.

NUMBER SIX
NOVEMBER 18, 2012

This dream carried Innocence and me, Embarrassment, to my mother's house. Innocence was helping cook dinner. I was helping Innocence cook some chicken gizzards. My two daughters had supposed to have gotten up early that morning and go to the barn to milk two cows. They were dragging around about it. I was trying to get them to go on and milk the two cows. Innocence began to put some medicine pills into her purse and I helped her. She was to leave and go home after dinner. Then I woke up.

NUMBER SEVEN
DECEMBER 19, 2012

My dream put me in a place where lots of people lived and worked. Innocence was there, so I kept seeing her; however, she was at a distance from me. There was a long bed, and several people slept in it at one time. All the people lay side by side when they were sleeping. I eventually lay down next to Innocence. We saw one another and recognized who the other one was. We were lying face to face, very close. We were now very glad of the other's presence.

Then I was going to paint a car, the one that Innocence and I had our last date in. The car was a 1959 red and white Pontiac Bonneville. Innocence needed a ride home, so I wanted to ask her if I could carry her home; however, I never did ask her before I woke up from the dream.

NUMBER EIGHT
March 14, 2013

This dream brought sadness to me. Innocence had died and the funeral or wake had begun. I saw her lying on a scaffold made from poles like the kind the Indians would burn their chief on when he died according to Western cowboy shows. Innocence was dead; however, at the same time, she was looking through the cracks trying to see me.

Then the dreamed changed. I was in a deep ditch. Then Innocence came walking down the road, and she was very close to me. However, I could not speak to her. I watched her as she passed by on her way to her house. I did find out where she lived. Dream ended.

NUMBER NINE
APRIL 17, 2013

In this dream, Dove (my wife) and I moved to a town. I do not know where it was. Across the street lived Innocence and her husband. They were living there before we moved into our house. We did not know that they were already living there across the street. When Innocence's husband found out that I, Embarrassment, had moved in across the street from them, he became upset and wanted to move someplace else. I had to convince him that I did not know that Innocence was living there before we moved in. Then he was okay with it. Then we four met together and talked. I could not hear what Innocence was saying. End of dream.

NUMBER TEN
APRIL 21, 2013

I dreamed that a number of people wanted to take Innocence's casket out of the ground so I could see her. A big part of the night they kept trying to figure out how to do it. I told them that I did not want them to do it; however, they kept trying to figure out a way. They finally found a way. When they opened the casket, Innocence was as beautiful as a teenage angel, as peaceful as a robin on a warm sunny, spring day. Dream ended.

NUMBER ELEVEN
APRIL 29, 2013

This time, I saw Innocence sitting in a red car on a hill slightly above me. The red car was turned crossways to me. She was sitting in the driver's seat, looking toward me. Innocence was waiting for the man that she was to soon marry.

I was returning back from town when she saw me. I asked her if she would still have me and marry me instead of the other man. Innocence said that she would. Dream Ended.

NUMBER TWELVE
MAY 19, 2013

Tonight I dreamed about Innocence again. In my dream, I saw her at a distance, and her daddy was also with her. They were near their car which was inside a very large building. The next day I went around the building and came inside where Innocence was sitting in the back seat of the same car. I got in and sit down by her. We never spoke; however, we both knew that we would finally be together. Innocence's daddy was in the driver's seat. He cranked the car and began to drive down the road. He knew that Innocence and I would now be together forever. She was young looking and beautiful. As we drove away together, I woke up.

NUMBER THIRTEEN
MAY 25, 2013

I had a bad dream about Innocence last night. She had gotten married. After about one week of marriage, she was kidnapped. The kidnapper put her in the back of a truck and drove very fast. The wind was howling loudly around her head and into her eyes. This caused complications with her eyes which finally killed her. A year or two later, I saw her husband. He was trying to find the man who had caused her death. Because he was married to her for only one week, he had learned very little about her personality and character.

Somehow her husband had heard that I knew Innocence before they got married. He asked me about her personality. I had the privilege to tell him about her inter warmth, joy, happiness, and purity. I told him how wonderful she was. I also shared with him of how her beauty was more than I deserved. Her purity of heart was as clean as an angel. Her love that would capture even a great king's heart. This I gladly shared with her husband. He never had the privilege of knowing her in all these ways. Dream ended.

NUMBER FOURTEEN
MAY 29, 2013

In this dream, my cousin found out where Innocence lived with a roommate. My cousin made the arrangement for him and me to visit them. When we arrived, we drove by the house the first time, but we stopped the second time around. My cousin went in first. Next I went in. Innocence took me by the hand and held on to it, giving me a welcome gesture. We stood close. She was glad to see me, but we never spoke a word to one another. We just kept looking at each other with joy-filled eyes and happy faces. Innocence appeared to be about 40 years old. End of dream.

NUMBER FIFTEEN
JUNE 4. 2013

I dreamed that Innocence died. Dream ended without any details.

NUMBER SIXTEEN
June 22, 2013

In my dream last night, I talked with Innocence. However, I do not remember the details, only that it was something that would help me. Dream ended.

NUMBER SEVENTEEN
JULY 12, 2013

Last night I dreamed about grave sites. Innocence was married to a friend of mine, and they both were dead and buried. Their graves were next to one another. I picked out grave plots for my wife Dove and me. The grave plots were lined up like this: 1) my friend, 2) Innocence, 3) Embarrassment, and 4) Dove. I did not want Dove to know where mine and hers were; however, I had planned to move mine and hers to the new area of the graveyard as soon as the new part was ready. Then we would be together in a different place in the graveyard. The graveyard was covered with beautiful yellow flowers. Dream ended.

NUMBER EIGHTEEN
AUGUST 27, 2013

I dreamed that Innocence sang at her own funeral. I did not understand the words; however, her voice was as beautiful as an angel. Her final message in song was well accepted. (Fare well, Innocence). Dream ended.

NUMBER NINETEEN
August 28, 2013

In this dream, Innocence had three automobiles wrecks. She would not turn in a picture report. Dove, my wonderful wife, died at this time. Then Innocence and I planned to get married after Innocence turned in the accident reports. I woke up.

NUMBER TWENTY
DECEMBER 19, 2013

This dream takes place in a very large auditorium. It had many long rows of circular seats. Innocence was sitting on the right side. I, Embarrassment, was sitting on the left side. I got up and went around the circle of seats and sit down directly behind Innocence. I then leaned forward and asked her if she would go with me on a date. She said that she would.

In the next scene, we were back in the same auditorium, sitting on opposite sides again. Innocence was again on the right side. I was on the left side. Again I got up and moved over to where Innocence was sitting and sit down directly behind her. I leant forward and asked her if she would marry me. The answer was yes. Then I moved one seat forward and sit down by her. I was very bashful and timid. I was very close to Innocence as I sat by her right side. I put my left arm around her shoulder. She then came closer to me.

After a short time in this position, it was announced over the loud speakers to all the people that Innocence and I were going to get married.

The scene changed to us riding down the road together in a car. We were sitting very close and Innocence laid her head on my right shoulder. I was driving the car and we were already married. While traveling down the road, we came up behind her daddy who was also traveling on the same road. He was going the same way on the four lane highway. While passing us, her daddy looked around at us from his car. Innocence and I turned our heads and looked at him as we passed.

Back to the second scene, while Innocence and I was sitting together, we talked to one another. However, I could not remember what we talked about. I woke up. End of dream.

NUMBER TWENTY-ONE
DECEMBER 23, 2013

Tonight at 11:15, I woke up from a dream about Innocence. Someone placed four pictures in my hand. One of them was a picture of Innocence. She could have removed herself from the picture and from my hand, forever, but she did not want to.

Someone suggested that we get married. So she agreed that we should. I heard her say that we should get married; however, I said that there was a problem with that. I was holding Innocence's hand, and she would not remove herself from the picture nor from me. She could have at any time. I told them that the problem with us getting married was that Dove and I were still married and living together so we could not get married.

At this time in the dream, Innocence removed herself from the picture and from my hand. It was sort of like she and the picture just floated out of my hand, but did not go very far from me. Then she came back to where I was. This time Innocence was not in the picture, but she was in the real as a person. She came very close to me and was going to wait for me. I could see her very plain and clear in the dream. She was sitting very close to me and was planning on waiting for me. At this time she was present as a real person, not on a picture. Dream ended.

NUMBER TWENTY-TWO
JANUARY 11, 2014

I dreamed that Innocence and I had a small, young baby. Dove and I were married and living happily together. Dove knew about the baby. Also Dove knew that I was the daddy of the child. Innocence had a job and was working; however, she became too disabled to work or care for her child. Only a few people knew that I was the child's daddy.

One day I saw Innocence holding her baby in her arms. She then almost dropped the child onto the floor. She was sitting directly in front of me, about two or three feet away. When Innocence began to let the baby slip from her arms, I reached out my hands and received the baby from her arms. This is when Innocence knew that she would have to give up her baby because she had no one to help her take care of her child.

Dove, my wife, wanted us to take the child and raise it. I then saw Dove holding the child, telling the child that she was the grandma. Dream ended.

NUMBER TWENTY-THREE
MARCH 2, 2014

In this dream, I was appointed administrator over Innocence's estate. She had passed away. At her death, I was to receive her inheritance. I had seen the check of the amount of $120,000 dollars. I did not know where the check was that was written to me. Innocence's daddy had already passed on; however, her mother was trying to get the money from me. I was trying to find the check because it belonged to me. I never found the check in my dream before it ended.

NUMBER TWENTY-FOUR
APRIL 5, 2014

This dream carried me on a hunt for Innocence. She was missing, and I had been looking for a long time for her. I went out into the woods searching for her. It was quite dark in the forest. I began to call her by name, "Innocence, Innocence, Innocence."

Then I found her daddy's grave. Next to his grave was Innocence's grave, but I kept calling her. She then appeared in my presence; however, she was very sick. Innocence was asleep at this time, so I tried to arouse her from her sleep. When she woke up, at first she did not want to have anything to do with me. She finally remembered who I was. Then she wanted to be close to me.

Innocence and I began walking in the dark woods together, but she kept a distance between herself and me. After a while, we stopped walking. At this time, Innocence was very sick, so she lay down on the grass. I went over to where she was and I bent down. I kissed her. It took a few minutes to get her roused up and realize what I was doing. Innocence got very close to me and wanted me to hold her tightly.

I knew that our time together would only last a few minutes longer. Then she would have to go back. Innocence kept holding on to me. I asked her if we had time for this. She said that we did have time. She desired to hold me close and rub on me. That was as far as we went with this. She began to slip from my arms and from my presence. It was time for her to go back to where she had just come from. I wanted to be with Innocence again even though it was only for a few minutes. As she returned back to her resting place, the dream ended.

NUMBER TWENTY-FIVE
APRIL 26, 2014

In this dream, I wanted for a long time to see Innocence again. I had known her for a long time before now. The problem was that Innocence was now dating someone else, someone I already knew. However, I kept looking for her. Finally I saw her one day and we talked. I do not know what the conversation included except that Innocence agreed to spend time with me.

After Innocence and I hung out together on a number of occasions, we agreed to get married. I could see her very clear and plain in my dream. I did not dream about a wedding actually taking place. Only that it did.

Then Innocence's daddy appeared in the dream. He was in the army and so was I. We were sharing an army bunk together. This is when I woke up. Dream ended.

NUMBER TWENTY-SIX
MAY 12, 2014

Last night I dreamed that Innocence died. I did not dream any details, only that she died. End of dream.

NUMBER TWENTY-SEVEN
JUNE 6, 2014

In this dream, Innocence had an envelope of pictures with her, but she did not want me to see them. One day when she was not there, her brother showed them to me. In the dream, we were in our early 20's. I could see her very plain in the dream. I said nothing to her when she came home that day. Innocence soon found out that her brother had showed me the pictures; however, she did not get upset about it. It was okay that I had seen the pictures. Innocence and I then talked, but I do not know what we talked about. Dream ended.

NUMBER TWENTY-EIGHT
JUNE 8, 2014

Last night I dreamed that someone had invented a phone that would permit you to talk to people from the past. I was trying to get Innocence's phone number of the past so I could talk to her. I got her number and was planning on calling her. Dream ended.

NUMBER TWENTY-NINE
SEPTEMBER 1, 2014

It was quite in our community. I was about to start dating Innocence. Then the young boys began to buy fast, red sports cars. They were very loud, inexcusable loud racket. Before I had the first date with Innocence, the dream ended.

NUMBER THIRTY
SEPTEMBER 12, 2014

This morning about 5 o'clock AM, I woke up. In this dream, there was a car pulling up in front of Innocence's house. I hurried around the corner of the street to see who was in the car. I wanted to see Innocence, but it was a man who stepped out of the car. This was a big letdown in my night dream. The dream ended.

NUMBER THIRTY ONE
OCTOBER 2, 2014

In my dream I was riding with a young boy in his car. He was gathering up food for a church lunch. There had been a lot of rain in the area. Gullies were washed out in the road and in people's yards. Getting to the church, we had to cross a large, deep pit of water. I told the boy who was driving the car that I was trying to find Innocence. He told me that at a certain time she would come walking across the wet mud pit to go to the church.

At the right time, I saw her coming; however, I did not recognize her. She looked much older than she was the last time that I had seen her. Innocence was walking through the mud. Then I called her by name, "Innocence." At this point, she stopped. I told her who I was and she recognized me. We hugged one another with mud all over both of us,

Innocence and me. The dream ended with us standing in the slimy mud embracing one another.

NUMBER THIRTY-TWO
OCTOBER 12, 2014

About 1:10 AM Sunday morning, I woke up from a dream where I had been dating Dove. We had been out on a date and were planning on going again to the same restaurant. I went ahead for some reason. When I arrived, Innocence was there planning to eat with me. She wanted me to marry her instead of Dove. Innocence cared a lot for me. In my dream, Dove also cared a lot for me.

When I arrived at the restaurant, Innocence came to my table and brought her plate. She did this so I would date her instead of Dove. When Dove arrived, she found me sitting at the table with Innocence. Dove was hurt because of whom I was sitting with. Then I got up from the table where Innocence was sitting. I planned to sit at the table with Dove. When I changed tables, this hurt Innocence. Each beautiful, nice girl wanted me to marry her.

What a hard place to be in? Trying to decide which heart I would break. Which one would I marry? I did not want to hurt either one. Three hearts in a tangle. It is hard to untangle the raveled thread. The pressure built up in my head and in my heart. Love was tugging at me from both sides. I was standing there between the two tables. I had never planned to get in this position. Dream ended without me never making a decision.

NUMBER THIRTY THREE
OCTOBER 17, 2014

In this dream, there were some people trying to find out how many children Innocence had given birth to. At this time, Innocence had already died. While the people were watching a small number of children run and play, they were observing how they responded under certain conditions. By this, they would know if they were or were not children that Innocence had given birth to. They decided that she had given birth to around six to eight children while she was living. Dream ended.

NUMBER THIRTY-FOUR
OCTOBER 24, 2014

I just woke up at 4:13 AM. In this dream, I had left the town and country where Innocence lived. I had been gone for several years. I finally came back to the community were Innocence lived. I wanted to see her but was too timid to go to her house.

One day I finally picked up the courage to visit Innocence at her house. When I arrived, there were several people in her house. Innocence was in a room by herself lying down long ways on a bed. I laid down crossways on the bed with her. I had my head above hers, and then I put my face to hers. I was looking into her pretty blue eyes. I then asked Innocence if she remembered me and knew who I was. She said that she did remember me. I then bent down and kissed her. She gave no resistance.

The scene then changed. I was driving a truck. I was on my way to pick up Innocence. The people in the area knew that I was going to pick up my girlfriend; however, they did not know who the girl was. When I arrived to the place where the group of people were, they were so surprised. They could hardly believe that I had Innocence with me. Some said that I could have chosen someone much better than Innocence. I was also asked why I had walked away from her. I told them that Innocence was the one that I loved and wanted. I never answered the question about why I walked away from her.

We hung around for a while. Then Innocence and I got in my truck and rode away. We went to some place where we could be alone. The people expected that we were going to be together. Dream ended.

NUMBER THIRTY FIVE
<u>NOVEMBER 18, 2014</u>

In this dream, Innocence was walking on a very busy street. She was on her way to her car which was parked nearby. This took place in a very large city. I was on the same street walking in the opposite direction. I was not noticing who I was meeting on the street. It was filled with many people going in all directions. As I passed by a person, we rubbed shoulders because there were so many people walking. As we rubbed shoulders, we both turned and looked back at the person that we had just made physical contact with. Innocence recognized me. I also recognized her. We then spoke and shook hands. I told her that I had wanted to see her again for a long time. She told me that she also wanted to see me for a long time.

The location where Innocence and I met was in an area where people were eating at a restaurant with outdoor tables on the sidewalk. In the crowd passing by was a group of ladies walking together. They were at a distance from us. One of the ladies was Dove; however, they immediately disappeared into the crowd. Dove did not see me, and this was the only time that I saw her in the dream.

Innocence and I started to sit at one of the tables and order something to eat, but we decided not to. Instead, we decided that we would go to Innocence's car and drive someplace together. We got in her large car and sat on the front seat. Innocence was going to drive. There was a long bridge in front of us that crossed a great river. We planned to cross over the river together, but the engine of the car would not crank. Innocence and I turned in the seat so we were facing one another. Not a word was said between us. We were just looking at each other. This is where the dream ended. I woke up at 11:45 PM Tuesday night.

NUMBER THIRTY SIX
January 28, 2015

This dream was very short. Innocence and I was trying to work things out to where we could spend time together. I do not know what the details were. Dream ended.

NUMBER THIRTY-SEVEN
March 9, 2015

I saw Innocence moving about in a crowd of people at her house. I was trying to get her phone number so I could talk to her for a few minutes. I finally got her number, but when I called she would not answer. I left a message for her to call me. I wanted so much to talk to her. I wanted to apologize to her for hurting her so badly. I wanted to ask Innocence to please forgive me.

Innocence was dating someone beside me. It seemed that it was a friend of mine, but I was not sure who he was. The driving force within me was for me to talk to her and get her forgiveness. I saw Innocence plainly but we never did get the privilege to talk; therefore, I would often go by her house so that I could get a glimpse of her. Most of the people who hung out around Innocence's house knew that I wanted to talk to her and wanted her to answer her phone. I was still trying to get her to answer her phone when I woke from my dream.

NUMBER THIRTY-EIGHT
MARCH 13, 2015

Innocence and I was in some kind of a building where it was very long but not wide. It was kind of like being on a passenger train where you walk from one train car into another one. You would walk from one room to another. I knew that Innocence was there some place. I went from one room to another trying to find her. After a long time, I finally found her. She was standing in a room. As soon as I entered it, I saw her. We were standing face to face. We began talking to one another; however, I do not know what we talked about. Where we met was in the bath room. There was no bad talk or unfit scenes. We were there just to talk. The bath room just happens to be the place where we met. We wanted to talk in private. That took a number of days to work out. We were still talking when I woke up. I do not know what we talked about.

NUMBER THIRTY-NINE
MARCH 22, 2015

I dreamed that Innocence lived in the country where I walked away from a long time ago. I finally went back to the area where Innocence lived. She often drove a small red plane on short trips.

I went out to where she lived and was able to come close enough to her where I could talk to her. I do not know what we talked about. We did not have a conversation about our past years of long ago. Innocence did tell me that she would spend some time with me.

I kept hanging around so she would come near me often. One day I did get to come close enough to her to where I was able to talk about something. I don't know if the people there knew that Innocence and I cared a lot for each other.

One day the people there were making big circles for some reason. She got into her red plane and made many circles around and around. She finally stopped. After her last circle she went home. I was there waiting for her arrival. We never talked at this time, even though she was glad that I was there. She looked very young, pure, innocent, and beautiful. Dream ended.

NUMBER FORTY
MAY 10, 2015

This dream carried me back to my old neighborhood where I was walking around. In my walk, I saw Innocence's daddy and we chatted. He remembered me. When I saw him, he was not at home. I kept walking down the street and passed Innocence's old home place.

There was a man sitting on her porch working on some musical instruments. As I walked past her house, he called me by my name. I then went to the edge of the porch. I was talking to the man who sit on her porch. I was going to ask him if Innocence still live there. About that time she walked out on the porch and sit down. She never said anything to anyone. I recognized who she was. Innocence appeared as a lady in her 60's or 70's. I never spoke to her. Dream ended.

NUMBER FORTY-ONE
JUNE 4, 2015

In this dream, Innocence was getting married, but not to me. I was told that she was going to accidently drop her engagement ring from her hand out of the window down to the ground. She would not know that I would be outside standing under her window. When it hit the grass, I was to pick it up then hand it to her. By doing this, I would get the chance to touch her hand. Also, I would have the privilege to talk to her again. I was standing under her window at the right time; however, as I looked up while she twiddled with her ring, her hands is all that I got to see.

The scene changes as it goes to where Innocence is going to be married that day. While she was waiting for the time to put on her wedding dress, she was laying on the ground underneath the corner of the mobile home that she had previously lived in. The mobile home was about 4 or 5 feet off the ground on the end where she was laying down. There were a small number of people there with her. I was standing about 12 feet from Innocence. She turned and saw me for the first time in a very long time.

She said to me, "We need to put this behind us."

With no details of what she was talking about, I agreed and said, "Yes, we do."

We talked together for a few minutes; however, I do not know what we talked about. Innocence reached out her hand for me to help her up from the ground. I responded by taking her hand and lifted her up to a standing position. I continued to hold her hand while standing very close to her. I could see her very clearly as I stood close to her. She was wearing a light colored blouse and a darker colored pair of slacks. She had long, light brown hair. As we stood close to one another at the end of the mobile home, we talked for a few minutes. I do not know what we talked about. While I was still holding her hand, she told me that later that day, after the wedding, she would see me and talk to me more. Then the dream ended with me standing close to her, still holding her hand.

Chapter Three

Journey to the End

In the Montana mountains near Hungry Horse Dam, Tim was traveling with his mother and father down a narrow, winding road. Studying the frigid February landscape, Tim snuggled against Shep's thick fur as he watched the falling snow outside the car window. To the right, an enormous mountain occupied the whole view, but leftward the vistas stretched for miles. Behind Hungry Horse Lake stood row upon row of white mountains. Snow laden tree limbs broke, sending resonant sounds resembling gunfire across the seemly peaceful valleys, occasional starting small avalanches.

Jerry Wells drove slowly on the road, slick as wet soap. The 1928 Ford had no heater and was missing a window. In the pane's place, the father had placed cardboard. Jerry's gloved hands tightly gripped the stirring wheel. The worn gloves had several holes, and his knee boots were torn on the side, one with a small hole through the sole. To combat the cold, Jerry wore blue overalls with an army-green overcoat, but he was still quite chilled.

His wife was little better off. Her brownish-gray checkered dress was made from wool, and a long blue coat, now faded, captured most of her body heat. Three pairs of socks and a pair of old tennis shoes kept her feet fairly warm.

Tim wore lined blue jeans and two shirts topped with a fur lined leather jacket. Gloves and boots fit tightly but still kept him warm. The cold did not seem to bother Shep, donned in her natural coat of brownish-white splotched fur.

"Look! There goes a deer!" shouted Tim, pointing excitedly. His parents looked, catching a glimpse of a young deer, baby spots still faintly visible through its reddish fur. The animal jumped through the snow, quickly disappearing into the forest.

"It's beginning to snow harder," observed Mr. Wells.

Gloria nodded in agreement. "Before it gets too bad, let's stop and dig some wood out from under the snow for a fire."

"I'm cold. Yes, us do. That will be fun," piped up Tim, holding Shep close.

Jerry pulled over at a parking place cut into the mountain side where tourists could have picnics during the summer. Aside from a couple of snow-buried tables and the straight cliff wall, the only other feature of the rest area was a tall evergreen tree standing like a mighty king with outstretched arms covered in snowy ice. The wind whistled under it, making Tim feel colder than before.

Father and son crossed the road and clambered down a small bank to a tree which had fallen months before. Jerry broke off rotten limbs with a small hatchet, then they carried the wood up the slippery slope to the road. The trip was difficult for the snow was nearly knee deep. After placing the wood on the frozen ground cleared by Gloria near the tall evergreen, they followed the new trail several more times until a good size pile of firewood rested beside the fire Gloria had originally started with an old newspaper.

Breathing deeply the pine scent rising from the flames, Gloria said cheerfully, "What a wonderful smell coming from the fire. Good choice of wood, Jerry."

Mr. Wells gave his wife a smile, loving her for finding good in the worst situations. Going to the car, Jerry opened the rumble seat and pulled out a fifty pound lard can for his wife to sit on. Tim received a water bucket, and Mr. Wells used a five gallon milk can. Gloria heated food over the fire. Warmth from dancing flames and hot food regenerated the family, creating a friendly atmosphere in the harsh winter scene.

Tim asked, "Mommie, can we sing some songs like us do at church?"

"Yes," she lovingly smiled at her only child. "What would you like to sing?"

The boy tilted his head, thinking. After a long moment, he responded, "'Comin' Home.' I like it."

Mr. Wells led the family as their loud voices filled the cold air with harmony, floating across the chilly valley until swallowed by the soft stillness of glittering flakes. The gentle presence of the Lord touched the destitute family as they sang from their hearts. With a faraway look, Shep lay close to Tim's feet, ears held erect, taking comfort from Tim's voice. She seemed to be thinking of something far away, something sad. As the last notes ended, Shep rose to her feet, trotted across the road and down the slope into the distance beyond.

"Daddy, can I go get Shep before she gets lost?" asked Tim.

Used to son and dog playing at various stops on their journey while the parents cleaned up, Jerry answered, "Yes, but don't go pass the tree at the end of our trail through the snow."

The child nodded his head and dashed away. He crossed the road and headed down the slope, stopping at the dead tree. "Shep? Here, Shep. Where are you? Come to me."

The wind began to blow from the northwest, sweeping swiftly around the mountainside, shaking snow from trees. The boy spotted the dog a few hundred yards down the mountainside where the slope became steep again. The boy called his furry best friend's name loudly.

The Wells began breaking up the tiny camp. Jerry placed the cans used for stools back into the truck of the car, while Gloria gathered up utensils and the leftovers from the meal. After she took her place on the frayed car seat, Jerry put the crank in place, rotating it. The motor remained quiet. Suddenly the man remembered he had forgotten to turn the key. He opened the driver's door, turned the key in its slot, then pulled the throttle with the spark down about one or two inches. Again he turned the crank and was rewarded by the motor sputtered to life.

While Jerry put the hand crank back into its place, the car went dead. "Always my luck," he mumbled. Fortunately the car sputtered to life after only one more turn.

Unnoticed, the wind had picked up, blowing snow off the large evergreen's limbs. The man raked snow from the windshield then from the side windows.

As he cleared the rear window, Mrs. Wells yelled above engine noise, "Jerry, you better go see about Tim. He's been gone a long time."

"Okay," the man replied. He had been too busy with his work to notice the quick approaching storm. Looking up from his work, he squinted through the fast falling snow. Visibility was only about one hundred yards. Walking to the edge of the frozen road, the father called, "Tim, come on. Let's go."

He waited for a moment in the peaceful scene of falling beauty. No answer. "Tim! Tim! Shep. Can you hear me?"

The only sound was the harsh wind blowing across the mountainside. A sliver of fear gripped the father's heart. "Tim! Answer me, Tim!"

The man looked back towards the cold fire bed. No one there. He glanced over the bank but the little trail was empty. No Tim, no Shep. Quickly Jerry rushed down the fast filling trail, stopping at the fallen tree. There was indentations in the snow were the boy had walked. The man followed but the blizzard quickly hid the tracks in the dimming light. The father called his son's name repeatedly, but the wind seemed to snatch the sounds before they exited his mouth. The mountainside grew steeper, and the man would have fallen several times if not for the trees he grabbed.

"Why did I let Tim go after Shep?" the man asked out loud in frustration. Faintly he heard his own name being called. At first he thought it was Tim, only to disappointedly realize it was Gloria yelling from the top of the road. Maybe Tim had already returned to the car.

Back up the mountainside Jerry climbed. For every two steps up the slope, he slid one step down. In the blizzard's fury, snow flew horizontal. The large evergreen tree in the picnic area bent nearly double, in danger of losing the battle with the storm every second. When the man finally saw his wife's stricken face, fear flooded his soul. Tim had not returned.

Shouting above the wind, Gloria yelled, "What are we going to do now?"

Heart pounding, Jerry stuttered, "We can't go after him. His tracks are covered." He paused, not knowing what else to say, his silent wife staring, near panic, eyes pleading for an answer. The man took a deep breath. "We pray."

Together in the howling wind, the couple held hands, beseeching God on their son's behalf. A supernatural peace swirled inside their souls, vanishing fear.

The husband finally said, "Let's find a house or town and ask for help." Not knowing what else to do, Gloria nodded her head, and the couple climbed into the still running car.

Tim continued downward along the steep slope, calling Shep's name. He slid more often than he walked, losing track of time and distance. The only thing which occupied the young boy's mind was finding Shep. Darkness came quickly in the rugged forest, causing the temperature to rapidly drop.

Suddenly the frozen ground ended, and the boy found himself falling. He landed with a jolt, screaming in fear. Snow cushioned the impact, protecting his bones. For a moment Tim lay quietly, realizing for the first time that he was in danger. He did what any eight year old would do—cried.

A furry creature appeared in the darkness, warm wetness licking the boy's tears. The child immediately stopped crying and wrapped his arms around the animal. "Shep! Where you've been? I've been looking everywhere for you."

The collie nuzzled the boy until he laughed, pushing her cold nose away. "Shep, we've got to find Mommie and Daddy. I'm cold." Though the dog could not understand the boy's language, she recognized the fear in his voice.

Tim wondered if his parents were looking for him. Surely by now the supper items would be packed and his parents ready to go. Sitting up with back pressed against the small cliff, he stared at the dark forest in front of him. Where were they? The blackness of the night seemed to be a living entity, unfriendly and cruel. Should he continue down the steep, slippery slope? What was at the bottom?

Pulling away from Tim, Shep whined and made her way upward through the snow for a ways. She barked a few times, but Tim would not follow. Coming back to the boy, she whined, pressing close against the child's body. She understood that the boy was in danger and knew the adult humans could help. Trembling, the boy rubbed her head. Uncertainty was a cancer of fear which kept him from moving. Shep gently took Tim's mitten hand in her mouth, pulling. Finally the boy rose, following.

The child kept up only for a short time. When Shep found a path heading upward through the rocky terrain, Tim slipped on bare rock, sliding ten feet before regaining control. The collie dashed to the boy, licking his face until he stood. Again the dog led uphill but the boy found the journey difficult and exhausting.

After falling for the fifth time, the boy stayed where he was. Tears rolled down his cold, red cheeks. "Mommie, why don't you and Daddy come get me? I'm lost. I can't find my way. There's no fire to warm me."

Shep whine, trying to make Tim rise. Realizing the child was too tired, she curled her body around him, offering what warmth she could. Taking comfort from her presence, the boy's tears slowly dwindled. Tim was only three years older than Shep, and he could not remember a time when she had not been part of his life. The two were inseparable. Where one was, the other could always be found.

In the cold darkness, Tim knew without a doubt that Shep would remain by him. He recalled the time when a large, brown snake was curled to strike him. Shep had run between him and the reptile, taking the bite instead. Mr. Wells had to rush her to the veterinary immediately to save her life. Tim had been listless during the long, endless days of Shep recovery at the vet's. When she had finally returned home, the two knew no end of happiness, playing together, running through blooming fields of cotton on their farm— now lost to the bank due to the Depression.

Shivering, Tim finally said, "Shep, we can't climb. It's too steep. Us go down to bottom of mountain. Maybe Daddy will be waiting for us there."

Numbly standing to his feet, Tim began the hardest journey of his young life. Together boy and dog half slid, half stumbled down the steep mountainside. Every time Tim fell, Shep was there to nudge him to stand again. Exhausted, body aching, Tim cried often—his tears turning to ice before reaching the lower part of his cheeks. The numb child did not notice that there was no longer feeling in his limbs.

Suddenly Shep barked, grabbing for Tim's leg. Too late. Snow caved in, carrying Tim off a thirty foot cliff. The child landed with a sicken thud, soften by a snowdrift. It was a long moment before the boy regained his breath. "Shep, where are you? Come to me. I hurt."

High above, Shep barked, her voice echoing in the darkness. The blizzard had almost blown itself out, and her voice carried loud and clear. It was some time before the dog could find a safe path downward. She bounced through the soft snow, barking every few minutes, yapping when she lost her balance and fell for a short distance.

Finally reaching Tim, she licked his face in reassurance. The boy slowly put an arm around the collie's head and buried his face in her long, coarse coat. In a strain voice, he manage to say, "Go get help, Shep. I can't go anymore." The dog whined, vainly attempting to make the boy rise. Tim pushed her face away. "Shep, go, please go. Find help."

His voice failed for his jaws were almost frozen shut. For a few moments, the collie lay beside the boy uneasily, sensing the child was growing too quiet. She knew they needed to reach humans—with warm fire and maybe hot food. Finally she rose, licking the boy's nearest cheek then dashed way. Making her way to the top of a high ridge, Shep sniffed the air, smelling no scents of humans. In the far distance, lights reflected off low, dark clouds. Between the collie and the nearest town lay Hungry Horse Dam and another icy mountain. Hopelessness filled the animal—the boy was hurt and she did not know how to save him.

In the quiet stillness which follows a snowstorm, Shep raised her muzzle into the air, howling her feelings of despair. Again and again she filled the night with her mournful cry. Across the valley, another animal answered her. Her ears perked up, but disappointingly she realized it was only a coyote. What help could he be? She howled again, holding the notes longer, pouring out the sorrow of her heart. There was no answer. Her cry could have been a great trumpet, but there were no humans to hear it. Far down in the valley, the town slept, not heeding the ringing cries of sorrow from the mountains.

Grieved, the animal clambered down the ridge to where Tim lay. He was cold and stiff. Whining, Shep pawed him, nudging his face. The only response was a faint grunt from the child. No longer could he wrap his arm around her neck or rub her head. Intense pain pieced her heart. Her boy was dying and she could do nothing to save him. There is no greater agony. She laid beside him, offering her only asset— body heat, but Tim's skin did not lose its blue hue. Shep placed her head across the boy's chest, feeling each breath he took, hearing every heartbeat.

The chest stopped moving. The drumming of the heart grew faint then died like a motor which cranks then sputters to a stop. The collie licked the boy's stiff face, whining. No response. From somewhere there was a faint light. Shep looked around hoping humans had arrived, but her nose reported no new scents. The light continued to grow brighter, and there were voices. Impossible. Her nose reported there were no scents.

Voices became closer, clearer, singing in musical harmony. Darkness melted away, and the snow turned golden in a dizzying light. The air seemed to be alive with thousands of voices singing joyfully. Shep's ears stood erect as she looked this way and that. Her eyes could only see the bright light and Tim's body, yet she knew they were no longer alone. The singing reached a climax then faded abruptly as if the singers had suddenly crossed a hill or threshold which blocked sound. The golden light disappeared, but in the peaceful circle of boy and dog, a lingering sweetness stayed in the air.

Shep did not understand what had happened. She only knew a long journey awaited her to bear the sad news. For Tim, his journey had come to its end.

Chapter Four

Walking, Walking Alone

The dark room was tiny, barely contained enough space for two and their supplies. The walls and roof were made from dried sage grass. There were no windows. The only light came from around the edges of a blanket that covered the opening which served as a door. A cool evening wind made the light blanket sway. It was a November wind, swift and harsh, for upon the great desert plain of Arizona, there was nothing to slow it down. Clouds gathered as the sun sunk low in the west behind the Castle Dome Mountains, painting the sky pinkish-orange. The occupants of the hut took no notice.

For three days and nights Jane suffered from a high, uncontrollable fever. Nothing her husband did seemed to help. Beside him on the dirt floor rested the now empty first aid kit, useless. Jim picked up a moist rag and placed it on his wife's feverish forehead. She moaned, twisting restlessly on the bed of grass covered by a thin sheet.

Jim studied his wife, noticing every detail. The white blouse with ruffles around the sleeves and collar had been a going-away present from her mother. She had held it up proudly and kissed the elderly lady on the cheeks. Now it was drenched in sweat. She had worn the long blue skirt the day she met Jim for the first time. Black hair ran in waves over her thin shoulders. Jim gentle brushed several strains away from her damp face. Unable to pull his hand away, he rested it on her flushed cheek. For a second her brown eyes opened, warm and caring. Briefly she smiled and clasped his hand tightly. He loved her, deeply and forever. Jane's body relaxed. Soon she was sleeping again. Jim pulled several blankets snugly around her for protection against the desert's night chill.

He went outside to tend the donkey which carried their supplies. Jim's tall body, muscular from a life of hard work, was outlined by the light of the newly risen moon. His tan shirt was loose fitting and tucked into his black buckskin trousers. Curly blond hair was cut short, and intense blue eyes peered from his handsome face.

The pack animal nudged his hand, looking for a snack, gentle as the elderly lady who sold them the animal. The woman had been bent and hobbled due to age, but her spirit shown. Hearing they were going to cross the great desert to deliver the Good News to the Apache, her wrinkled face had lit up as she recalled stories of the Indians she had met. They are good people, she had said, honest with their trading. Long have she prayed for someone to live among them, to be a witness. After selling her only animal to the couple, she gave them extra food and water for the journey, advising the best path and the locations of the few springs. As Jim refilled the canteens, he was again thankful for the elderly woman. They never would have found the tiny rivulet of water which flowed from the base of a large boulder if not for her advice.

Entering the tiny hut, Jim felt like he was inside a prison which trapped his love from fresh air and sunlight. He had hurriedly constructed the hut to protect Jane from the desert heat when she could no longer travel. They were half way across the plain when she began having chills then fever. Her body ached, but never in any one place. Both had thought a day or two of rest would return her to normal, but three days later she was worse. Her fever rose and fell like a roller coaster, climbing to a dangerous high that morning. Only in the last two hours had it finally dropped. Determination lined his face. Tomorrow he would take Jane out to see the sunrise.

Jim seated himself on the hard ground beside his wife. For a long time he watched the blankets move upward and downward with Jane's breathing. Becoming restless, he let his mind wander down lanes long since traveled. He enjoyed reliving the good times in his life. He pulled on those memories during hardships, finding strength to continue, counting his blessings.

His childhood had been happy but fleeting, coming to an abrupt end when both his parents died in an automobile accident. New York City can be a lonely and scary place for a shy fourteen year old. The few relatives he had were either in Ireland or out West. For three weeks he stayed home, depressed and afraid. When the food and rent ran out, he hit the streets, living in dirty alleys. He tried to find work, but there were not enough jobs available for grown men, let alone a lanky teenager. Eventually a restaurant manager hired him to carry out trash and wash dishes. But loneliness drove him back on the streets where he joined a gang. There was nothing else to do. He smoked cigarettes and marijuana, later becoming addictive to cocaine. The greatest excitement in his life became dodging cops by running through alleys carrying stolen goods with his buddies. He was nearly caught a time or two, but he no longer cared.

Three years he lived on the streets. Sometimes at night he found himself longing for something he could not name, could not understand. It was a feeling, a void, like something was missing. He tried to avoid thinking about his parents, knowing they would be shocked to see what he had become. His childhood haunted him, a shadowy reminder that once he had known love and laughter.

Late one evening he finally found what he had been seeking. Walking along a narrow street lined with blooming trees, he heard distant music. Curious, he followed the sound which was somehow familiar. Turning a corner, he spotted a small stone church with a slender steeple on top. Jim entered the building and took a seat on the back row, listening to words from his childhood when all had been safe and innocent.

"What can wash away my sin, nothing but the blood of Jesus," the people sung heartily.

Jim gripped the pew in front of him tightly. He was tired of the heaviness which seemed to always weigh on him. He remembered Sunday school lessons and Bible stories. And his parents faith.

Jim was never the same after that day. He left the church with a new light in his eyes. He promised God that he would quit the gang if he could find work and a place to live. The next day, he was offered a job at a boarding house, receiving free housing for maintenance work.

Jane opened her eyes and in a hoarse voice whispered, "Jim, darling, I need some water."

Quickly her husband opened a canteen and held it up to her lips. She sipped the cool liquid, then fell back into a shallow sleep. The last two days she had been alert, but today she only slept. Jim rubbed her arms. She did not respond. He poured water on a cloth and bathed her face, remembering when they had first met.

He and a friend had been traveling on a train bound for New Jersey. Jim was going to stay over the Christmas holiday with his friend's family. Jane boarded the train halfway through the trip and sat across from Jim. A light conversation was struck but deepen when they both realized the other was from New York City. She laughed at his jokes and smiled at his stories, but it was not until he spoke about his faith in God did her eyes light up. She spoke about her own desire to be a missionary to the Indians. An hour later when Jane got off at her stop, Jim had fallen helpless in love. After Christmas break, he 'accidentally' found himself in front of her home. For the next hour, he paced numerous times pass the two-story house, trying to work up the courage to knock. Suddenly around the street corner she appeared with a brother and sister in tow, all three clothed in warm coats and holding packages. His heart skipped a beat as she neared. Recognizing him, Jane greeted him warmly and invited him in.

Two years later they were married. They attended a tiny Bible college, studying intensely the known cultures of the Indians, focusing on the Apache tribe in Arizona. Too little was known. Evenings Jim worked in a factory and Jane was a part time secretary. They saved every penny possible, but money was slow in coming and bills needed to be paid.

One night stood out forever in Jim's memory. After a long, tough day of labor, Jim was greeted by Jane wrapping her strong arms around his neck and asking, "How much money do we still need for the trip?"

"About twenty dollars," Jim answered, calculating in his head. "It'll take about another two month to get."

Jane suddenly began to weep, a look of wild joy dancing across her face.

Confused, Jim took her hands. "Why are you crying?"

Through tears she softly spoke, "Today I was visiting a home of a couple. I told them of our plans, hardships we must overcome, and our burden we feel for the Apache. To my surprise, they wanted to know more about our great and perfect love. Before leaving their home, they had pledged themselves to our Master and given me one hundred dollars for the trip. Oh, darling, what a blessing this is!"

In shock, Jim sat down. "Thank God. He has blessed us beyond ours greatest dreams."

"Yes! We can leave tomorrow." Jane laughed joyfully, spinning around the room.

Looking back, Jim recalled they had gone to sleep that night rejoicing, completely at peace.

Finished washing Jane's face, Jim walked outside again. High above, an owl flew across the dark sky. The bird was free, having no worries or responsibilities. In seconds, the animal was out of sight. A few dark rain clouds gathered in the northwest, but would unlikely come this far south. Stars sparkled across the blackness, distant and cold. What would this long and lonely night deliver to us, the husband wondered.

"Jim. Jim, darling, where are you?" Jane's soft voice slipped from the grass hut.

Quickly he entered. "How are you feeling, my dear?"

"Better." She gave him a smile, the same one she used the day she invited him inside her home for the first time.

"I am so thankful," he whispered.

"Is there anything I can eat?"

"We have plenty of food and water. What would you like?" He answered gently.

"A bowl of soup and water would be great."

As the young woman ate, Jim felt hope stir. It was the first good meal she had taken in two days. He talked about whatever came to mind, the beautiful moon, the antics of the attention loving donkey. He promised to take her outside tomorrow to see the sunrise. Jane pretended all was normal, even laughed as he described a bat which overshot an insect it was aiming at and almost hit a cactus. But in her eyes was the haunting shadow of lingering pain.

After eating Jane drifted back to sleep, leaving Jim alone with his thoughts again. The harshness of the trip came back to him. They had taken a train as far as possible then bought horses. Several weeks later their horses were stolen, and they continued by foot. It was slow going. In more settled areas, kind-hearted people heading to nearby towns, offered rides in their wagons. The couple traveled through scorching heat and rain. Once they were caught outside in a hail storm. Land became less populated and wilder. Each day brought small miracles and dangers.

It was especially difficult for a young city couple who knew little about outdoor life. But they had learned. For a short while, they joined a wagon train, picking up many tips and develop strong friendships. Unfortunately, the caravan was headed in a different direction. Sadly they said farewell to new friends and headed southwest. They were exhausted but hopeful when reaching the village where the old lady sold them the donkey. Talking with her had encouraged them, preparing them mentally for their hardest challenge. Spending the last of their money on the animal and fresh supplies, they had started out across the broad desert, excited that the end of the journey was near.

Jim awoke suddenly, jerked from troubled dreams. He listened to the stillness of the night, wondering what had awakened him. Jane moaned and twisted on her bed of dry grass. He reached out a hand in the darkness and felt her skin. It was hot and sweaty. He lit the lantern and moistened the cloth again. Though he bathed her face and arms repeatedly, her temperature continued to climb dangerously high.

Opening feverish eyes, she asked, "Darling, listen. Do you hear music?"

Perhaps someone was passing close by. Hoping against reason, Jim sprung up and exited the hut. Outside the cool night breeze blew gently across the sand. An owl hooted in the distance. To the north was the dark bank of lifeless mountains. In the east lay the great desert plain of lizards, cactus, and craggy rocks. Heart pounding, Jim looked southwest. The view only revealed more dry land, chilled and dead.

"It is beautiful, so beautiful." Jane's frail voice seemed to come from a great distance.

Fear gripped Jim's heart. It came like a sly serpent sliding through short stubby grass at night. He could not shake loose from its bite. He was alone and his wife was becoming worst. How could he tell her that there was no one? That she was hearing things? In the distance a coyote howled. Several answering calls resounded through the night air. He shivered, feeling no comfort from the cool night air. It seemed to surround him like a ghost from an old haunted house.

As despair overwhelmed him, quiet words whispered through his mind from the Holy Book. *Perfect love casts out fear.* Perfect love. God's relationship with man. Lectures from college drifted back to Jim when he needed comfort most. His breathing slowed as peace filled him. God had protected him when he was an angry youth living in the streets and brought him from the gutters to college, given him a wife as beautiful on the inside as she was on the outside. God would not forsake them in the middle of a desert.

Jim entered the hut. Jane did not move. He placed a hand on her forehead, now cool and damp. She had fallen into a deep sleep, her breathing becoming more regular. He lay on the ground beside her and slept.

As the sky lightened, the howl of a coyote woke Jim. For a moment he listened to the mournful sound. Other coyotes answered, their sad cries piercing his heart like a sharp sword. Quickly he sprang to his feet and knelt beside Jane, his eyes taking in her still body. Gently he touched her cold cheek, calling her name several times, but she did not respond. She felt cold and still. Gently he kissed her firm lips, tears running down his cheek, splashing onto her face.

An emptiness filled him. Once again he was the fourteen year old orphan alone in a huge, uncaring world. Without dreams, without vision, without hope.

"God, how could you take her?" His throat constricted in anger. "Why? Why Lord?"

Often quoted words whispered silently through his mind. *Yea, though I walk through the valley of death, I will fear no evil, for you are with me. Your rod and staff, they comfort me.*

Jim repeated the words several times to himself. God was still with him, loving and protective. He sensed the presence of God's Holy Spirit overshadowing his heart in a wonderful way. Needing time to gather his thoughts before saying a final goodbye to Jane, he slowly turned and walked out of the grassy hut.

He was only a few steps outside when he heard a voice say, "Jim, darling."

He quickly turned and entered the hut. To Jim's excitement, he saw Jane sitting up and smiling. She had felt the touch of the Holy Spirit and death had fled, leaving behind life, joy, and peace.

Jim and Jane continued their journey together. Jesus walked with them, directing their steps to fulfill the great calling. Jim did not have to walk alone for Jane walked alongside him.

Chapter Five

Poems

Broken Relationships

Where did you leave your relationship and love?

In a desert so dry
In a forest so dark
In a for granted valley

On a mountain of busyness
In a stream of neglect
In a fire of jealously

How many lonely and empty miles
Lay between your spouse and you

It is not good that man (woman) be alone
Do not leave him (her) in the darken valley
With loneliness and emptiness

Hear his (her) cry for you

Genesis 2:18— And the Lord God said, It is not good that the man should be alone; I will make him a help mate for him.

Desert Trails

The trail has been dusty
And the sand burns my feet
O' someone with some water
I wanted so much to meet
The desert is so wide
And this trail so very long
It seems that my soul
Has almost lost its song

Since traveling this desert trail
Months and years has gone by
Often I stop and ponder this path
Because my heart aches and cries
If I had someone to walk with me
We could together sing a song
Since I left that last mountain
I walk this trail alone

Somewhere in the past
Jesus would pass by so near
Now if I could feel his presence
On this desert trail so drear
I know he has not left me
It is I who took a turn
Onto this lonely dusty trail
For your presence, Jesus, my soul yarns

As I stumble slowly on
A thorny cactus pricked my skin
The cactus tried so hard
To poison my soul with sin
There are a lot of desert creatures
Who tried to bring me down
Who tried to make me fall
While swiftly circling round

The trail has been so weary
As I pressed on each day
By night the darken creatures
Tried to turn my soul astray
They would whisper in my ear
There's no end to this trail
Then I heard the Holy Spirit say
Everything will soon be well

Then morning broke that sunny day
The sun was in the sky
I looked beyond the desert trail
And saw a mountain high
I sprang up so quickly
And toward the mountain I ran
Before I hardly knew it
I was out of the desert sand

I rushed upon the mountain slope
With excitement in my eyes
To my amazement
A cool stream was flowing by
And quince my thirsty soul
Then lifting my eyes toward heaven
Saying you helped me reach my gold

No more will I wonder
So far away from God
Because it pains my soul so deeply
As I walked the sin path of sod
My desire is to daily walk
With Jesus every day
So, God, please help me
Never to turn the wrong pathway

Wedding Gown

Revelations 9:7-9

Jesus, the bride groom is coming
And I know it won't be long
He is coming to take his bride
To her brand new home
For she will be there with him
Very, very soon
The bride has made herself ready
For the coming of the groom

I have never seen a bride so beautiful
All dressed up in white
Her wedding gown has no blemishes
It is lovely and so bright
Not a spot or wrinkle anywhere
Can be found
Oh, she looks so lovely
In her beautiful wedding gown

The smile on her face
Shows the love in her heart
From her faithful bridegroom
She will never, never part
There's excitement in her voice
As the groom is looking down
Oh, she looks so lovely
In her beautiful wedding gown

As she stands there looking
Up into the sky
She cannot hardly wait
To tell this world good-by
Her ears are now listening
For the trumpet to sound
Oh, she looks so lovely
In her beautiful wedding gown

I'll Serve You Lord

In this life, I found salvation
And I know it was meant for me
Through Christ my Lord
I got a glimpse of glory
On that bright, shining shore

Oh Lord and Savior, up in glory
I long to be by thy side
To love and worship through the ages
And to dwell in heaven on high

In that bright city where the lamb is the light
And there will be all day and no night
Where there are no tears
And streets are pure gold
And they say there we will never grow old

I'll serve you Lord as long as I live
If it be a million years
I'll keep remembering
For ever and ever
I'll serve you Lord as long as I live

Little Lord Jesus

The little Lord Jesus
Who slept on the hay
Has ascended to Heaven
My sins he washed away

And now I am so happy
I rejoice and sing
For the little Lord Jesus
Is now my King

Wise Men Seek Jesus

Nicodimus was a man
Who came to Jesus in the night
He was a man who well knew
The wrong from the right
But he needed someone to save him
And to make his heart right
Therefore, he came to see Jesus
In the darkness of the night

There was a man named Legion
Who lived among the tombs
They bound him with chains
But he breaks them very soon
Then one day he met Jesus
As he walked down the road
Jesus saved and delivered
Him from his heavy load

Early that morning as day was breaking
Mary came, her heart was aching
She wondered who might roll away
That heavy stone that early day
But to Mary's great surprise
Jesus surely did arise
Jesus spoke to her alone
Her heart was glad, her faith was strong

Wise men seek the Lord
When their hearts are sad and blue
They know that no one loves them
And cares for them like you do
Wise men seek the Lord
Wise men find him to
Won't you open up your heart
And let his love shine through

Don't Let My Brothers Fall

Thou hast brought thy children in
Thou hast delivered them from sin
And thou hast kept them through the many years

Trials has come and has gone
Don't let them stand alone
Don't let my dear brothers fall

Love thy neighbor as thyself
Is what God's Holy word says
And our brothers we're to love them all
Lift them up and for them pray
Lest thy brothers go astray
Don't let my dear brothers fall

Jesus lights the pathway
For my brothers who have gone astray
I can see that their love has grown cold
And they stand at hell's door
Don't let them sin anymore
Don't let my dear brothers' fall

Don't let my brothers' fall
Don't let my brothers' fall
In thy arms brace them strong, dear Lord
For the storms of life has come
And temptation will be strong
Dear Jesus, don't let my brothers fall

Memories of Mother and Daddy

Memories of my parents are precious to me
All the hard times, all the good times I can see
Memories of my parents that is filled with love
I thank God they now rest in heaven above

Memories of Mother while she was young and strong
Labored so hard, days were so long
She cooked, ironed, and mended our clothes
Each stroke filled with love, lightened her load

Mother looked ahead with each smile and tear
While as she walked with us year after year.
She taught us to share, to love, and to give
That we might through life happily live

Memories of Daddy will always last
They happily fill my mind, and then leave like a flash
Memories of Daddy as he plowed in the field
They seem as a dream, but they are very real

Daddy turned the soil and planted the seed
While he was loving and caring for me
He was a man with courage, who looked to the Fall
That he might be able to buy shoes for us all

Memories of my parents are precious as gold
They may become dim, but will never grow old
So I bid them farewell, but not for long
For I plan to join them in our heavenly home

Cloud of Honor

One beautiful and lovely day
My Lord will come again
Upon the cloud so beautiful
Get ready my dear friend

The honored cloud will receive him
When he is coming down
He'll stand upon the beautiful cloud
And not upon the ground

Upon the cloud a shout will ring
That will be heard across our land
Then the dead in Christ will rise
And with him we shall stand

Some cloud will be honored
Will be honored some lovely day
When Jesus comes to take his bride
And take his bride away

Have No Sorrow Or Regret

I have no sorrow or regret
For me when I am gone
While my family is so sad
I'll be shouting around God's throne
When the day of parting comes
Their hearts will be so blue
Thank God, praise you, Jesus
I'll be in heaven with you

When we come into this world
Life has so much to give
Lots of joy, lots of tears
And a strong desire to live
But what matters most to me
Is Jesus in my heart
Love for him, for family
A love that will never depart

As I walk down life's pathway
I found a reason to live
As I experienced salvation
That Jesus so freely gives

The joy he put into my heart
The peace that now is mine
Makes me love him more and more
And helps my life to shine

Now I come to journey's end
My life has been so great
I want to go see Jesus
I can hardly wait
Jesus now is calling me
And I must bid fair well
The ship has raised her anchor
She's now made ready to sail

Don't expect me to come back again
Into this world of sin
When you get on board to join me
Raise your sail high into the wind
Then we will meet together
On that beautiful shore
We will then be together
On heaven's shore forever more

Willing To Go

Willing to go
Willing to stay
Lord Jesus, help me be willing to go
That your love I may share
And your grace I may show
Lord Jesus, help me be willing to go

Lord I ask you today
Please don't take my burden away
Lord Jesus help me be willing to go
Lord don't remove your great call
To you I give my all
Lord Jesus help me be willing to go

In the field or across the plain
May I share your precious name
Lord Jesus help me be willing to go
Over the mountains or across the sea
Sharing your word, setting men free
Lord Jesus, help me be willing to go

There may be joy, there may be tears
As I work through the years
Lord Jesus helps me be willing to go
I must gather the golden grain
In the sunshine and in the rain
Lord Jesus, help me be willing to go

Lord, while with you, I walk so near
And the path is made so clear
Lord Jesus helps me be willing to go
And if your call should come to me
May I be willing to follow thee
Lord Jesus, help me be willing to go

One Faded Rose

(In Memory of Edsel Savell)

As I walked down the dusty road one day
There upon the hill
I saw a small rose bush
And it stood there quietly and still

I said to the bush
That stood among the grass and weeds
You must get pretty lonely
Need pruning and have other needs

Kneeling down by the little bush
I pulled back the weeds and grass
So that it's short and rough limbs
I would not break and mash

Saying to the thorny rose bush
That stood alone on the hill
I will carry you down into the valley
And plant you in the rose field

As I listen with my heart
The contented rose bush seem to say
I am happy here on the hill
Please do not take me away

I don't want to live among the roses
The garden so beautiful and big
I like it here on the hillside
Beside the road, on the ridge

To the little rose bush, I said
If you grow alone in this sand
You may be noticed by only a few
And seldom touched by a soft and tender hand

O, said the joyful rose bush
I might bring joy to one
I might make someone happy
As I grow here quietly in the sun

I stood, and walked quietly away
Knowing the little rose bush was content
Down the slope onto the road
And down the patch I went

Many times through the summer
Down this path I trod
Upon the hillside, I saw the bush
Growing among the weeds and sod

From the heart of this broken bush
There among the thorns
Bloomed a beautiful rose
With peddles soft and warm

This delightful and lovely rose
Rejoiced my summer days
I watched its leaves fall
And its bright blossom fade

Late in the autumn, I noticed
As I was walking by
That the rose had fallen
And the rose bush had died

The rose did not grow in the valley
But it blossomed here on the hill
Touching the hearts of those passing by
As it grew there quietly and still

I stood there thinking about Jesus
And wondered when he's making heaven's bouquet.
Maybe he gathered this rose
And tenderly carried it away

To bloom in God' s garden
Forever there to be
In his new home
Happy, rejoicing and forever free

As I walked away that day
When it was time to go
My heart had been touched
By this one faded rose

Our Father Chose A Lamb

Death was near God's family
And something had to be quickly done
Our heavenly Father said, "I'll choose a Lamb
So that victory can be won"

Our Father loves his family
And for death to be stopped
A Lamb had to die
From our Father's flock

This Lamb had to die
There upon the tree
Shedding his precious blood
For all of God's family

Our Father walked out there
Way out into the field
Down by the cool brook
Just beyond the hill

There among the beautiful Lambs
He began to look
Surely there is one worthy
That could be took

He looked among all his flock
Among the cherubim and angels so bright
Trying to decide which little Lamb
Would be sacrificed that night

After much searching
Among all the sheep
Every one of them
Our Father wanted to keep

When Father was about to leave
Turning to his side
He saw a little Lamb
Who was trying to hide

Father said, "Little Lamb
Come near to me
I am looking for a perfect Lamb
And you I want to see"

The little soft Lamb tip-toed
Over by our Father's side
Oh, this touched Father's heart
And he wanted to cry

Father said, "I see no spot or blemish
In your wool any place
I have chosen you little Lamb
To share my love and my grace

He took the Lamb up unto his arms
And hugged him very tight
Saying, "It won't be very long
Until everything will be alright"

Our Father knew that very soon
He must tell his little Lamb goodbye
So when he turned his head away
He began to cry

Slowly He bowed his head
In much grief and pain
And said, "I love you Jesus"
You know, Jesus was the little Lamb's name

He hugged the little Lamb
And rubbed him on his head
The Father knew that very soon
His lovely Lamb would be dead

He said, "I'm sorry little Lamb
I love you with all my heart
But very soon from Heaven
You will have to part

The little Lamb looked up
As to say, "I understand I must go"
As though he understood
What our Father wanted him to know

Father gave the Lamb another hug
And said, "I must send you down among men
There they will kill you
By an evil and wicked hand

He put the Lamb down
In a narrow little trail
Father said, "You must be on your way
But everything will be well

Come, Holy Spirit,
With this little Lamb you must go
All the way to the earth
For the trail you already know"

When the Lamb came into this world
Our Father was looking on
The heavenly host of angels
Gathered to sing a song

Time went by swiftly
And many days had gone by
The day of sacrifice came
It was time for the Lamb to die

He stood there in humility
In much pain and woe
But to the rugged cross
He knew he had to go

As the Lamb hung there on the cross
A host of angels stood silently by
When it was time to give his life
Our Father turned away his head and cried

Oh, the pain in Father's heart
So strong and so sharp
From His dear little Lamb
Life must depart

Soon the Lamb's body
Lay silently and still
In the cool, dark tomb
Way upon the hill

But suddenly from the tomb
Came a great sound
The guards lay as dead men
There upon the ground

A voice from an angel
So loud and so clear
Said, "He has arisen
He is not here"

To our Father's side
The Lamb will quickly go
Then victory will be forever won
And the whole world will know"

Oh, how our Father rejoiced
When his little Lamb came walking in
Victory had been won
Over death and over sin

Father called everyone in
And said, "Quickly come and see
My favorite little Lamb
And what he has done for me"

Then Father took a stroll
Out across the field
Down by the silent brook
Just beyond the hill

With the little frisky Lamb by his side
While walking in the Field
Victory had been won
There on Calvary's hill

I'm so glad Father chose a Lamb
For his big family
Now we will all be together
For all eternity

What Will The Last Chapter Have To Say?

When Jesus takes out his paper and pin
To write the last chapter of your life
When you have lived many good years
And it is time for you to die
Will it make Jesus happy
When he writes the last pages of the book
Or will it bring tears to his eyes
When he takes the final look

Your life is being written in heaven
Being recorded day by day
And all the things that you do
And about all the things that you say
He writes on the pages when you go to church
And all the many times you kneel and pray
All the times you sing and laugh
And all the times that you play

In the book of heaven
He records all of your life
Whether you live in peace with men
Or live in trouble and strife

If you visit your neighbor
And tell him about God
He will record the love that you shred
And about the path you trod

But what about the crooked deal
That you gave to your friend
And remember the lie that you told
God's word tells us that it is sin
If you allow the devil
To catch you in his hook
This also will be recorded
Yes, recorded in heaven's book

You see each chapter is being recorded
With detail and great skill
And when you stand before your God
The book, your life will reveal
The pages will be open
On that great judgment day
Will He say enter in
Or will He turn you eternally away

All the good deeds we do
Cannot open heaven door
If we want to make it in
We must not sin any more
When you have lived your life
And it's coming to a close
May you be to our Lord
Like a sweet smelling rose

In heavens great record book
What's recorded on the page
Good or bad, which ever it be
Will determine through the age
The place announced by our Lord
Where we spend eternity
The decision made according to the book
Whether eternally bound or set free

What will the last chapter have to say
What will the last chapter have to say
When He has taken his last look
And slowly close the book
What will the last chapter have to say
What will the last chapter have to say

How Will I Answer God When He Calls?

Will I receive his great love,
That is sent from heaven above?
How will I answer God when he calls?

Will I from God swiftly flee?
Quickly hide behind the trees.
How will I answer God when he calls?

Will I be made clean,
In the red crimson stream?
How will I answer God when he calls?

Will I bow down on my knees,
Or make aprons of leaves?
How will I answer God when he calls?

Will I bow my head in shame,
Or lift up his holy Name?
How will I answer God when he calls?

Will I say this life is mine,
For you, Lord, I have no time?
How will I answer God when he calls?

Will I say "Here am I,"
And bid this world goodbye?
How will I answer God when he calls?

When he needs someone to preach,
And he needs someone to teach.
How will I answer God when he calls?

When the trumpet shall sound,
And I am laying there in the ground,
How will I answer God when he calls?

When I stand there at his throne,
Will I be pleased where I have gone?
How will I answer God when he calls?

Show Me The Field

Lord, you tell me, the harvest field is great
And so many people just sit around and wait
They say they are waiting for a better day
Not realizing that time is fast slipping away

Lord, tomorrow never comes to your children so many
They tread on Holy Ground and enjoying a life of plenty
While the harvest is white and the wind take it away
They say, Lord, be patient, I'll work another day

Lord, I have wasted many precious days
I have labored for comfort, in my own way
Now I lift my eyes and gaze across the field
I see many souls perishing, Lord, show me your will

Lord, the harvest fields are white and very great
Show me the pathway that I must quickly take
Lord, there are so many fields that I could choose
Show me the right one, so that not one soul will I loose

Lord, I can work in the valley where the souls are so low
I can work on the mountain where the great harvest grows
I can work on the hillside where the seeds are sown
Wherever I work Lord, do make me very strong

Lord, show me the field that I must work in today
A field that is white and ready to be gathered away
With my hands I'll labor and gather the ripe wheat
So that they, Lord, with you will be ready to meet

Lord, may I always work and labor my very best
Until harvest is past and the sun sets in the west
Lord, show me and make it very real
Show me where to work in your harvest field

Prayer

Show me the field, Lord, show me the field
As I work for you and do your will
Lead by your Spirit, make it so real
Show me the field, Lord, show me the field

Church Closed

I was in church the other night
When I heard the preacher say
We will close the church down
For this next most Holy day
There will be no one here to preach
And no one here to pray
Because we are closing the church down
On this next most, Holy day

What if a poor blind man
Came tapping slowly along
He could not go any farther
He was not very strong
When he did reach the church house door
This is what the sign did say
We have closed the Lord's house
On this most Holy day

Down the road came a cripple
Barely dragging along
Hoping to hear a prayer
And maybe a gospel song
His heart was heavy burden
And his spirit sank very low
Because into the Lord's house
He was not able to go.

Sorry, my friend
There's no one here to pray
We have closed the Lord's house
On this most Holy day
Come back at our conveyance
Is what the sign did say
Come back another time
And then with you we will pray

One came looking for Jesus
Early this most Holy day
Thought he would find him there
As he stumbled along the way
The Lord was nowhere
Where he could be found
Because on this most Holy morning
They had closed the church house down

The last one that came by
Had often been told
That here he could find water
For his dry, thirsty soul
But he had to turn
And sadly walk away
Because of the sign on the door
We are closed on this most Holy day

Gathered By An Angel

*(Dedicated to David and Romadee Whitmire,
Douglas' uncle and aunt)*

In the presence of God's Holy Spirit
And a pen in my hand
I am thinking of two special flowers
Planted by God's desire and command
Two flowers so beautiful
And filled with God's eternal love
Flowers who are very special
To me and our savior above

In the bright and warm sunshine
On this peaceful, splendid day
I walked through the flower garden
Out on the hill here to pray
As I turned about and looked down
Across the rolling, gentle slope
I noticed a tiny yellow flower
And it moved about with many strokes

The little flower was full of life
It was very easy to see
For just a moment there
I thought it was looking back at me
Standing there in the bright sunshine
Being touched with the cool breeze
This soft yellow flower
Moved silently with freedom and ease

Then I turned about slowly
Looking to my right
Quickly a frisky blue flower
Came into my sight
Upon its tiny little arms
Rested a beautiful butterfly
Reflecting God's tender care
From way up in the sky

To my left, there on the hill
I saw this flower, snowy white
I believe it had just opened its eyes
Sometime during the night
Then the wind touched this sleepy flower
And in the garden would not let it stay.
It moved away so swiftly
As though an angel gathered it away

Yes I know that our Lord
Out here on the hill
Has planted his own flower garden
Here in the field
I believe that Jesus
Walks by, so very near
When his flowers bloom
Year after year

Most of these beautiful flowers
Go unnoticed by man
Even though God planted them
With his tender loving hand
These colorful soft flowers
Grew close to you and me
However we rush through life so swiftly
Their beauty we seldom take time to see

Here in God's flower garden
Where I kneel to him each day
Among God's beautiful flowers
I lift my voice and pray
I think God for his blessings
And for all the lovely flowers too
Flowers of many colors
Orange, purple, yellow, white and blue

While silently waiting here on the hill
Among all the beautiful flowers
I have been here quite a while
O, maybe even for hours
I am now thinking of two
Faithful flowers of honor and might
That has bloomed for many years
Through the day, and often in the night

These two flowers are my kin
And very dear to me
Their life has been beautiful
In Christ, joyful and free
Among God's choicest flowers
They stand tall and strong
They have bloomed like the many flowers
In this life full and long

O, but like the silent flowers
Standing there upon the hill
I walked among them many times
Not noticing their love that is very real
Many times these flowers may have longed
For a visit from their kin
On occasion they would come by
And often Jesus would drop in

Well, it's time, I must go
Back across the field
Down the steep slope
To the valley beyond the hill
O, but to these two flowers
I really do love you
I appreciate your life's beauty
And in Christ your faithfulness too

My prayer is for you
Two precious and beautiful flowers
That you will be gathered by an angel
In your closing hours
To be planted in God's choice bouquet
To bloom on that heavenly shore
To blossom eternally before his throne
And to rejoice with him for evermore

Walking In The Dark Forest

Many years ago I walked through a great, dark forest
As I walked through the forest so dark
I was attacked by a great beast
That lived in the dark forest

I called out for help
I cried in hurt and pain so many, many times
It seemed no one could hear my cry for help
And come to rescue me

After I was wounded for many months
Being crushed inside over and over again by the beast
I thought maybe no one will deliver me
Out of the paws of this beast

One night while being pressed down
By this great beast
Tangled in his web
Someone heard me cry in pain

To my surprise
Through the darkness of the forest
Approached a great lion
With a mane thick and full

In a moment with one swift blow of his paw
He wounded the great beast
And drove him out of the dark forest
To never roam there again

Many years has gone by now
I should feel safe walking through the forest
Knowing that the beast cannot wander there anymore
Yet there is a fear that rises up to trouble me

I should be able to walk through the forest
And touch the trees without being afraid
When I look at the forest I see the trees
It is I that I do not trust

The trees are gentle and kind
Nice to me
However I do not fully trust myself
As I now walk through the forest

The lion is there to protect me
From the beast
But now when I walk through the forest
I must not come in contact with the trees

Because I do not fully trust myself
As I walk in the beauty and quietness of the great forest
For this reason, I keep a distance
Between me and the beautiful trees

Maybe the time will come
When I can walk through the forest
That I'll be comfortable touching
The beautiful trees and enjoy my walk again

Baby's Silent Grave

*Inspired by three unmarked graves
belonging to author's aunts who died as infants.*

I found on a quiet and peaceful hill
A young child's silent grave today
My mind went back years ago
Where some mother knelt to pray

This mother remembered
As she knelt there on the ground
How Jesus had received her beautiful baby
And had given to her an eternal crown

Mother held the child tender and close
The last moments on that day
She had rather given her own life
Than for her baby to have been taken away

But the call had been given from Heaven
The Lord was calling her home
Oh, the pain, the hurt, the emptiness
Mother felt all alone

As the angel reached out his hands
To receive this lovely child that day
It may have made the angel weep
As he took the child away

But, oh, the hurt in mother's heart
Angels may never know
As the child was taken from her arms
It was time for her to go

Mother was standing there weeping
As her child was laid to rest
It seemed that her heart would fall to pieces
She had loved her child her very best

She felt she could not go
Another sad and lonely day
Then she remembered it was Jesus
Who had received her child that day

Mother looked beyond the grave
To her Lord up on high
Then she was able to let go
And tell her baby goodbye

The last trip mother made
To that peaceful, silent grave
She remembered that someday
Jesus would come, the baby to raise

Mother will join her baby
At God's holy throne
There in heaven with Jesus
Mother and baby will be together at home

Yes, memories filled my mind
As I stood there on the hill
Knowing Jesus will open the silent grave
By his Spirit, His power, and his will

Happy Birthday, Sister
Your First Day

Dedicated to Alma, Doug's sister

The sun was really hot
On the last day of June
Only two or three hours
And it would be high noon

We were down past the spring
Gum pulpwood we had to peal
Waiting for dinner time
So we could share a meal

While we were cutting trees
And working very hard
Grumbling and complaining
And feeling very tired

Down the hill came my daddy
He had walked half-a mile
Dad approached so quietly
And wore a happy smile

We all stopped working quickly
Turning in a whirl
Dad said, mom's got a baby
And she is a little girl

Up the hill we rushed
Laughing as we went
To see the baby girl
That the Lord had sent

Soon we reached the house
Hurrying into the room
To see the baby girl
Born the last day of June

We were all so happy
It could have been a boy
To see a little girl
It filled our hearts with joy

Years have passed so quickly
Life has served us well
I love you little sister
This I gladly tell

When all of life's paths
You have finally trod
May your last step be
From earth, to heaven with God

Happy birthday, little sister

Creator Of The Mountain

When you're in the darken valley
And it's hard for you to see
You look upon the mountain
And there you wish to be

But there is one thing you must remember
In the valley as you walk through
The creator of the mountain
Created the valley too

Sometimes in this life
When we are walking through
Life gets so heavy
I know not what to do

Down here in this valley
It's hard day by day
I have learned to call on Jesus
I have learned how to pray

I keep hoping that someday
That I can climb that mountain high
It looks, oh so easy
As it reaches toward the sky

But there's someone in this valley
Who is telling me no
I know he's the Holy Spirit
And he won't let me go

It was not upon the mountain
Where the blind was made to see
Where the lame was made to walk
Where Peter walked upon the sea

So down here in this valley
I believe I'll surely stay
Working for my Jesus
Until he calls me away

When you're in the darken valley
And it's hard for you to see
You look upon the mountain
And there you wish to be

But there is one thing you must remember
In the valley as you walk through
The creator of the mountain
Created the valley too.

My Friends Of Long Ago

I had Jesus as my friend
When I was just a lad
He helped me to be good
And not to be so bad
When I grew older
And finally became a man
I kept Jesus as my friend
He guides me by his hand

I use to run and skip about
With all my closest friends
Now I lift my weary head
And see my journey's end
They use to fill my heart with joy
As we would run and play
But now I long for my friends
My friends of yesterday

Where are my friends
My friends from long ago
Who said they loved me
And it seemed to be so
Today I need a friend
On whom I can lean on
I look here and there
But my friends are all gone

Time has taken my friends away
And left me here all alone
Some have moved far away
God has called others home
O my friends of yesterday
That I use to know
I long to see my friends again
My friends of long ago

As I sit here in this rocking chair
Just rocking the long days by
O I feel so sad and lonely
For a friend to drop by
If one would kindly drop in
Only for just a little while
It would thrill my heart so much
As he shared his time and a smile

When I get to heaven
If the Lord gives me a rocking chair
I may sit on the porch and rock
0, may be for a thousand years
So I can talk to all my friends
My friends I use to know
I will sit and talk a while
To my friends of long ago

Inspiration For Poems

BABY'S SILENT GRAVE

One day while I was visiting an elderly cousin of mine, she showed to me three unmarked graves. They were sisters of my mother. My mother never told me that she had the three sisters. This made them my aunts on my mother's side.

As I stood there on the hill by the road, it began to trouble my mind. Three graves with no grave markers and there were no names to remember them by. My kin, my family, would be forgotten after one or two more generations.

The thought began to bother my mind. I began to think about the mother who had laid her babies there to rest on the hill by the road. From these thoughts came the poem, "Baby's silent grave."

BROKEN RELATIONSHIPS

In relationships, one or the other often draws away from the other and leaves him or her very much alone. I was putting some questions out before my readers so maybe they will stay close to their real love and not neglect them. Genesis two, verse eighteen, the Lord said that it is not good that the man or woman should be alone.

CHURCH CLOSED

The first verse of this poem tells of words that I actually heard a pastor tell his congregation. He said that they were calling next Sunday's service off. When I heard this, I could not believe what I just heard. Closing God's house on a worship day, I had never heard of that before. My mind could not get peace over this until I pinned these words, "Church closed."

CLOUD OF HONOR
One day while I was outside looking at the beautiful clouds, this thought came to me. My mind began to guide me in the direction of this beautiful cloud of honor.

CREATOR OF THE MOUNTAIN
One summer I carried our oldest daughter to Gatlinburg, Tennessee in order for her to do mission work for the summer. When I was leaving her there, I drove to the top of a mountain overlooking the city. We got out of the car to look at the beautiful view. While I was standing there the Lord began to give me these words. Living in the valley can be a good place to work for our Lord.

DESERT TRAIL
I was thinking about lots of hardships that we bring on ourselves. Also, why does it take us so long to get back on the right track in life? There is help, but often we pass it by. Why?

DON'T LET MY BROTHERS FALL
This is a prayer for our brothers and sisters. This poem lifts up our request to the throne of God because we love our brothers and sisters in the Lord.

GATHERED BY AN ANGEL
This poem was dedicated to my uncle and aunt, my mother's brother. The two special flowers represent my uncle and aunt. They were two very special people and very kind. I compare them with flowers growing in God's big flower garden way out on the hill. The garden was a great place to go and pray. This couple was growing in God's flower garden and were very close to him each day.

The Holy Spirit gave me these words as I wrote the poem. I knew that one day, the Lord would come and gather these two beautiful flowers and carry them home with him and he did.

HAPPY BIRTHDAY, SISTER

My sister is the only girl born into our family. She was the baby of seven children. We were so excited when she was born. I wanted to tell her in a special way that I love and appreciate her. So I thought that I would tell her about the day that she was born. These thoughts led to this poem to tell her Happy Birthday, Sister.

HAVING NO SORROW OR REGRET

I was pondering the things that I have done for my Lord. I have no regrets; however, there is much more that I could have done. Also I was thinking about the day when Jesus calls me home. We should enjoy our life here as we live for the Lord. When Jesus calls us home, we should not try to delay. In Psalm one hundred and sixteen, verse fifteen, the Bible says "Precious in the sight of the Lord is the death of his saints." Be ready is what I was thinking about.

I'LL SERVE YOU LORD

While thinking about our service to our Lord and what heaven will be like, I had these thoughts come to my mind. We need to serve him for as long as we live.

LITTLE LORD JESUS

This short poem came about while I was listening to the song "Away in the Manger." Because Jesus is no longer in the manger, where is he now? The Lord put these thoughts together in my mind. So Jesus is now my Savior and my King forever.

MEMORIES OF MOTHER AND DADDY

One day I was thinking of some of the things that my parents had done for me. I thought about tears and smiles that they shared with us. How they gave themselves to hard work and sacrificed for us. So I wrote about them in this poem before they slipped from my mind.

MY FRIENDS OF LONG AGO

I was lonely one day and thinking about my friends. No close friend had stopped by in a long time. I wished so much that at least one would drop in for a visit. This poem sprang out of these thoughts of me being lonely.

ONE FADED ROSE

This poem is about my first cousin. He and I ran around together when we were growing up. After attending his funeral, I began to mediate on his life. I could not get it off my mind until after I had written this poem about him. My cousin in this poem is "The Rose Bush." As he grew older, he did not become popular or famous. However, he seemed to be content with the life that he was living. Like the rose bush on the hill in the poem.

As I walked away from the cemetery that day, I can honestly say, my heart and life had been touched by this one faded rose.

OUR FATHER CHOSE A LAMB

What brought about this poem were thoughts in my mind that I just could not dismiss until I followed the Holy Spirit in writing the words to the poem.

I had recently preached a sermon from Exodus, Chapter Twelve. These verses tell us that the Father of every family was to take from his flock a lamb. The lamb was to be killed so his blood could cover their sins. Also the first born child would not die when the Lord passed over the land of Egypt.

With these thoughts on my mind, The Holy Spirit reminded me that our Heavenly Father also took a lamb from his flock. The lamb that he chose also had to die so that our sins could be washed away. The lamb that our Father chose was named Jesus.

SHOW ME THE FIELD

Several years ago, as I was wondering what the Lord wanted me to do for him, the Holy Spirit gave me this poem. I knew that he had a field for me to work in. I did not want to miss it. The Lord did show me the field and I thank him very much.

WHAT WILL THE LAST CHAPTER HAVE TO SAY?

I was meditating on the end of a Christian's life. I began to wonder what God might write on the last pages of our life. From this book we will be judged. Whether our deeds were good or bad, we will have to give an account for them. I wondered if what he has to record in his book will make Jesus happy or bring tears to his eyes. People ought to give serious thought about what they believe and why.

WALKING IN THE DARK FOREST

I was reflecting on my past life and some of the things I went through after I became an adult. This poem may be harder to understand than some of them. In this poem, the great beast is Satan. The great lion was Jesus. The forest represented people as a whole. The trees are the individuals, namely females.

WEDDING GOWN

I began to compare Jesus and his bride, the church, with an earthly wedding. We made weddings so beautiful and lovely. Thinking of this, I began to write about the groom Jesus and his beautiful bride. Oh, she looks so lovely in her beautiful wedding gown. Refer to Revelations, chapter nineteen verses seven through nine to reveal about the wedding gown. I hope you are wearing the wedding garment.

WILLING TO GO

I wanted to go where Jesus wanted me to go. Also I knew that it might not be easy; however, whatever might be the cost, I was willing to go. I saw a harvest field white and ready to be gathered. With the harvest field ready to be harvested, I told myself and the Lord that I was willing to go then came forth this poem.

WISE MEN SEEK JESUS

While driving in southern Florida one day, my wife and I saw on a bill board the words "Wise men seek Jesus." As I thought on this sign, the Holy Spirit began to put the verses together for me. I was thinking on Bible characters, and it all came together how we need to seek and find Jesus.

About the Author

Douglas Townsend was born a country boy and still loves the rural forests, hills, and fields of Mississippi.

In 1969, Douglas became a minister. After he graduated from Southeastern University, he was ordained in 1974. Over the years he pastored churches in three states and had a radio ministry for five years.

After his retirement, he continues to be active teaching Bible studies, gardening, and occasionally writing.

www.ingramcontent.com/pod-product-compliance
Lightning Source LLC
Chambersburg PA
CBHW051255170626
46809CB00004B/1652